JEWISH RESISTANCE IN WARTIME GREECE

This publication was made possible
through a grant from the
John S. Latsis Foundation

Jewish Resistance in Wartime Greece

STEVEN BOWMAN
University of Cincinnati

VALLENTINE MITCHELL
LONDON • PORTLAND, OR

First published in 2006 in Great Britain by
VALLENTINE MITCHELL
Suite 314, Premier House, 112–114 Station Road,
Edgware, Middlesex HA8 7BJ

and in the United States of America by
VALLENTINE MITCHELL
c/o ISBS, 920 NE 58th Avenue, Suite 300
Portland, Oregon, 97213-3786

Website http://www.vmbooks

British Library Cataloging in Publication Data:

A catalogue record for this book has been applied for

ISBN 0-85303-599-7 (cloth)
ISBN 0-85303-598-9 (paper)

Library of Congress Cataloging-in-Publication Data:

A catalog record for this has been applied for

Printed in Great Britain by
MPG Books Ltd, Bodmin, Cornwall

Contents

List of Plates

Foreword

In the history of twentieth-century Greece, a period that continues to attract the interest of scholars and non-scholars alike, is the decade of the 1940s. The violence, destruction, and human suffering of those terrible years undermined every national institution and social group and brought to the fore new forces, conflicts and aspirations that, inflamed by external influences, shook the state to its core. The decade's momentous developments are by now well known and the subject of countless publications: the Greeks' victory and Mussolini's humiliation in the Albanian war, the Nazi invasion and the collapse of the Metaxas regime under the impact of the dictator's sudden death and military defeat, enemy occupation under German, Italian, and Bulgarian forces distinguished only by the degree of their brutality, widespread famine, national resistance, the rise of the populist left, the virtual eclipse of support for the monarchy, escalating internecine violence, post-liberation political crisis and economic floundering, foreign intervention, and, finally, full-scale civil war. Each of these developments had its distinct cast of characters, causes, dynamics, and consequences and needs to be studied separately as well as in their cause-and-effect relationship and in their totality. Despite the many excellent studies, much work remains to be done.

The resistance movement in enemy-occupied Greece has been the subject of many books by participants, eyewitnesses, writers of various ideological leanings, and scholars. Except for memoirs and personal accounts, the vast majority of publications chronicle the historically significant events and the role of the principal actors, domestic and foreign, their organizations and military operations, and the impact of resistance activity on the public at large. This is history from the top down, in which the various leaders receive attention while ordinary people remain almost entirely faceless and anonymous, their involvement and fate expressed in aggregate numbers.

Recently, scholars in Greece and abroad have begun a systematic investigation of the resistance movement at the ground level: village, neighborhood, extended family, individual fighter. This history from the bottom up, or micro-history, seeks to answer questions that so far have remained unresolved or the subject of unsubstantiated speculation. For example, beyond the well-known leaders and their lieutenants, who among the ordinary citizens joined the resistance and why? Patriotism and the wish to fight the foreign occupiers may have been an overarching motive but is hardly a sufficient explanation. Many patriotic Greeks remained passive, convinced that resisting the forces of occupation was futile, that enemy reprisals were too high a price to pay, and that Greece had already sacrificed enough in the war to defeat the Axis aggressors. Some thought that resistance activity played into the hands of the communists, whom they came to fear as much as the foreign enemy. In deciding to join the resistance how important were considerations of partisan politics and ideology, the need to escape from the occupation authorities, or the desire to settle personal scores? What factors determined which resistance band one joined, and how free was the choice? Why was so much violence at the local level directed at fellow Greeks? What is the connection between wartime resistance and the ensuing civil war? As careful research and analysis of the evidence provide answers to these complex questions, the pieces of the puzzle begin to fall into place and our understanding of the 1940s becomes more complete and profound.

The harsh deprivations, wholesale uprooting, and sheer brutality of the enemy occupation affected virtually all Greeks, but especially the middle class and professionals, resulting in appalling loss of life. Death from starvation, epidemics, executions, and other forms of violence were particularly prevalent in the German and Bulgarian zones and, after Italy's capitulation in the fall of 1943, across the entire country. Yet perhaps the single darkest event of the four-year ordeal was the systematic destruction of the Greek Jewish population.

Despite occasional and mostly localized signs of anti-Semitic behavior, the vast majority of Greeks had come to regard their country's Jews as compatriots and a vital element of the nation's human assets. During the occupation a broad spectrum of Greeks, including the collaborationist government in Athens, protested the introduction of anti-Jewish measures by the Nazis in 1942. Some Greeks sought to hide their Jewish friends and colleagues or help them escape to safety. Several thousand Jews found refuge in mountainous areas controlled by resistance groups. Nevertheless, of a total of about 75,000, some 60,000 Greek Jews perished, mostly in extermination camps in Auschwitz and Treblinka. At the war's end, the country's Jewish population had dwindled to fewer than 10,000. The large and centuries-old Jewish community of Thessaloniki, which at the beginning of the twentieth century accounted for almost half the city's population, was virtually wiped out. For Thessalonians young and old, in the early months of 1943 the sight of their Jewish neighbors and playmates being herded to the railroad station and the awaiting cattle cars etched indelible memories of horror and despair.

Although the available literature on the virtual destruction of Greece's Jews is extensive, answers to important questions await a more detailed examination of the evidence, especially at the local and individual levels. Among them are questions that relate to the intersection of two distinct but interconnected subjects: the fate of the Greek Jews and the Greek resistance movement. For example: once the impending danger to the Jews became apparent, did the resistance organizations actively encourage Jews to seek protection in guerrilla-controlled areas? If so, when and how? Which resistance groups were more aggressive in this regard and why? Why did relatively few Jews take advantage of the opportunity to escape to the mountains? What factors and characteristics distinguished those Jews who did join the resistance? What was the actual contribution of Jews to the resistance movement? These and related questions are the subject of Steven Bowman's new and engrossing study.

The interaction between Greek Jews and the wartime resistance is a subject that poses especially difficult problems for researchers. A veil of secrecy surrounds both parts of the topic. The surviving records of the principal resistance organizations, such as EAM/ELAS, EDES, and EKKA, are meager, patchy, and not likely to prove useful on issues that were admittedly not of high priority, such as the recruitment and sheltering of Jews. British and American wartime intelligence reports are helpful but hardly plentiful; they also deal in aggregates and the overall situation, not with individual cases. Most of the existing evidence has to be gleaned from memoirs, recollections, and interviews conducted years after the war and is at times little more than personal accounts or hearsay whose reliability may suffer with the passage of time. Cross-checking and verifying such accounts is rarely possible. Moreover, for Christians and Jews alike, involvement in resistance activity was extremely dangerous not merely to themselves but to their entire families. Accordingly, secrecy and the concealment of one's true identity were essential for survival. There was widespread use of false names, nicknames, and *noms de guerre*, creating a deliberate smoke-screen that to this day makes it difficult to determine whether a particular resistance fighter was Jewish. Given the dangerous times, it is to be expected that Jews might not wish to reveal more than their identity as Greeks.

A leading authority on the history of the Greek Jews and of the Holocaust, Professor Bowman is keenly aware of these problems in researching his subject. He presents impressive new evidence, much of it collected from interviews he conducted himself with Holocaust survivors. Yet he concedes that at present a comprehensive history of the Jewish participation in the Greek resistance movement cannot be written and that much work remains to be done. To his credit, he regards his new book as a contribution to that ultimate goal and an attempt to establish its historical framework, as well as an opportunity to present sketches of heretofore unknown individual cases of Jews in the ranks of the Greek resistance. In this he succeeds admirably.

Indeed, Professor Bowman has adopted a broad view of resistance to the enemy. In addition to guerrilla activities in the mountainous regions of Greece, he presents information concerning the involvement of Greek Jews in urban resistance, in which the principal objectives were sabotage operations and the collection of military intelligence. He also devotes a chapter to the truly heroic performance of Greek Jews who, deported to Poland, found themselves in Warsaw's ghetto. A number of them managed to join the Polish underground in the Warsaw uprising and met their death reportedly fighting under a Greek flag. At Birkenau, the notorious extermination center linked to the Auschwitz concentration camp, several hundred Greek Jews were executed for refusing to operate the crematoria. Predictably, an attempt to stage a revolt had an equally tragic end. Such little-known chapters of the destruction of Greece's Jews make this volume highly readable and add to its historical value.

Concerning the participation of Jews in guerrilla activities on the mountains of Greece, which remains the principal focus of his research, Professor Bowman's new findings are potentially quite significant. Thus, although the Greek Communist Party's Moscow-trained leadership did not include Jews, there were leftist Jews among the tobacco workers who gravitated toward the party in the interwar period. Of the many Jews who served with the Greek armed forces in

the Albanian war some joined the nascent resistance immediately following Greece's formal surrender. There also appears to be a connection between the mass deportations from Thessaloniki in mid-1943
and the decision of Jews to flee to the mountains to join guerrilla bands.
By far the vast majority of them, numbering in the hundreds, served
with the communist-led ELAS, while only a handful are known to
have gone to the anti-communist EDES.

These are important findings that shed light not only on the tragic
fate of Greece's Jews but also on the character of the resistance movement at its base. To be sure, some of the evidence presented here calls
for further investigation, fuller analysis, and more detailed explanation
of underlying causes of events and of human motives. Thus Professor
Bowman's on-going research adds significantly to our understanding
of a major turning point in recent Greek history and points the way to
what remains to be done. For those who lived through the events he
describes, it also revives painful memories of what the entire Greek
nation endured in the darkest hours of the Second World War.

John O. Iatrides
Professor of International Politics
Southern Connecticut State University

Abbreviations

AHEPA   American Hellenic Educational Progessive Association
AJDC   American Joint Distribution Committee
AMM   Allied Military Mission
BEF   British Expeditionary Force
EAM   Ethniko Apeleftherotiko Metopo – National Liberation Front
EDES   Ethnikos Dimokratikos Ellenikos Syndesmos – National Republican Greek League
EEE   Ethniki Enosis Ellas – National Union 'Greece'
EKKA   Ethniki kai Kinoniki Apeleftherosis – National and Social Liberation
EΛAN   Ethniko Laïko Apeleftherotiko Navtiko – National People's Liberation Navy
ELAS   Ethnikos Laikos Apeleftherotikos Stratos – National People's Liberation Army
EPON   Eniaia Panelladiki Organosi Neon – United Panhellenic Organization of Youth
ETA   Epimelitia tou Andarti – Guerrilla Commissariat
KKE   Kommounistiko Komma Ellados – Communist Party of Greece
OSS   Office of Strategic Services
SiPo/SD Sicherheitspolizei/Sicherheitsdienst – Security Police/Security Service
SIS   Strategic Information Service
SOE   Special Operations Executive
UNRRA   United Nations Relief and Research Association

Preface

The story of the Jews in the Greek resistance during World War II is as much a part of the general story of the Holocaust in Greece as it is integral to the story of Greek resistance to the Axis occupiers. Without the German conquest of Greece, there would have been no occupation, no persecution, no resistance, and Greece might have been spared the subsequent vicissitudes of civil war that poisoned its culture and retarded development for the next generation.

The Holocaust as it affected Greek Jewry is sufficiently represented in the scholarly and memoir literature, even if it has yet to be integrated into the broader story of that tragic period. While recent work on the Holocaust has updated the documentation and revealed new aspects, most scholarship on its impact in Greece still relies on Molho's history – first published in 1948.[1] That sad story, alongside which this volume is a separate treatment, is told elsewhere.[2] Rather, the emphasis of this book is on the virtually unknown story of Jews in the Greek resistance, a story that since the war has been only partially explored.[3]

The necessity for such a book hints at one problem Jews faced during the war. There is a long-standing tradition among Greeks that Jews did not fight (at least since biblical times), and aside from Jewish memory there is little discussion of their role in the war or the resistance in the literature.[4] A corollary to this silence is the fact that most Jews who survived in the mountains or hid in the cities identified themselves as Orthodox Greeks. Hence neither they nor Greek scholarship has noted their participation. For the record, which this book attempts to redress, Jews did fight during the war and during the occupation. Their contribution to Greece should be noted in the literature and it should also become part of the story of the Jews during the war, a story that is otherwise dominated by the terrible tragedy that included the near total destruction of the Jewish communities of Greece.

It should be emphasized that such an enquiry by no means detracts from the participation of the rest of the Greek population that served in or aided the general resistance. We shall have some references to the various groups of Greeks and non-Greeks as well as the ideological and gender facets of that movement in the course of the following chapters. Rather, here we should look at two perspectives on the subject that are somewhat related and even have reinforced each other due to the dreadful fate of the vast majority of Greek Jewry.

The most salient point to note is that Greek Jews suffered a loss of nearly 90 per cent of their prewar population. That tragedy, for all its consequences for Greek and world Jewry and its important – if neglected – place in the Holocaust, tends to support long-term assumptions about the Jews as victims. These assumptions, of long tradition and ideologically based, were instituted by and manifested in both Christian Roman law and Islamic *shari'a*. Both legal systems reflected the religious attitudes of their respective cultures toward the Jews from whom they had adopted their monotheism and with whom they were in competition for the claim to be God's Chosen People. The Jews lost that competition due to the aggressiveness of Christians and Muslims, who between them conquered the western climes from Afghanistan to the British Isles. Both Christians and Muslims inherited the degradation of the Jewish citizens of the Roman Empire to   second-class citizenship in the lands and societies that preserved the Roman legal tradition. The Church too, in all of its diaspora throughout the oekumene and its modern successors, continued to function as the bureaucratic heir of the Roman Empire, which had recognized its legality and gave it authority. Hence the Church – and here I include both the Catholic and the Orthodox branches – continued to preach contempt for Jews even as it defended the (limited) rights of Jews according to the Roman law that defined Judaism as a permitted religion.

One of the consequences of the Christian Roman legal tradition was the exclusion of Jews from military service. As non-combatants Jews were naturally considered contemptible by the military classes of Christian Europe, who defined reality and status by the sword.[5] In the less civilized West, where the Germanic tribes who imposed their military and tribal culture for the next millennium and a half monopolized fighting, the minority of Jews had to be protected against Christian zeal by papal order and the reality of their usefulness to the conquerors. Later, in the thirteenth century, the King's Peace of the emerging new monarchies put Jews, alongside male and female clergy,

outside the society of violence that defined feudalism. Islam too prohibited non-Muslims from military service. The difference between
Jews and Christians in the world of Islam was that Jews did not have
the availability of independent Christian arms to support any rebellion
or threaten intervention in the case of mistreatment.[6] The last Jewish
revolts against Islam came from the heavily populated Jewish centers
in Iraq and Iran in the late seventh century. Henceforth non-fighting
Jews would be treated with even greater contempt as passive *dhimmi*, a
contempt that turned to hatred once Jews regained their national independence and an army to defend their homeland after World War II.

Therefore it is not strange or unimaginable that European and
Islamic literature also treat with contempt and even satire the Jew who
did not fit into the military mindset that characterizes these two
realms.[7] Although the American and French revolutions opened modern society to the idea of Jews undertaking military service, the
entrenched military classes in Europe and even in the United States
(albeit for additional reasons), continued in many circles to reject
extending any honor to Jews. Even so many of the new states that
emerged in the two centuries following both revolutions officially
welcomed their commitment and active support. Jews flocked to the
armies of Germany and other new nations as a badge for their nationalism. The preceding remarks are of course a generalization that must
be tested and proven in the case of each new nation since one of the
major problems of the nationalist revolution was its attitude toward the
Jews who were treated as the 'other' and were more often than not
unwelcome.[8] The researcher into attitudes toward and treatment of
the Jews will find considerable rewards in the revelation and clarifica-
tion of the various factions that constitute the social infrastructure of
power in modern states. While Jews served in the army, and even
excelled, to prove their right to the gift of citizenship, there remained
a segment of the military that denied them, to as great an extent as
possible, the same right, let alone privilege, to serve as did the majority
(Christian) population. A similar process was at work in the Ottoman
realm after the Jewish *zimmis* were liberated to serve in the army.

How much more so was this the case during World War II? There
resistance was divided along a fault line that defined the civil war in
each country. Each country was divided not only between those who
supported the Axis and those who opposed it, but also among those
who denied the legitimacy of the conquerors, where there was a fundamental difference between – to put it simply – the Left and the

Right. The socialist or communist supported Left mostly welcomed Jews among its supporters and fighters while the Right, reflecting political or religious conservatism, more often than not eschewed Jewish support. And in certain cases, Poland for example, the right wing of the resistance even assisted the Holocaust of the Jews by fighting against Jewish resistance groups or killing individual Jews when the opportunity arose.

So the victimization of the Jews in the war has tended to supersede in historical memory the participation of the Jews in the armed conflict.[9] So much so was this a shocking realization among survivors that the biblical phrase – 'like sheep to the slaughter' was applied out of scorn and guilt to the victims. Yet over half a million Jews, for example, fought or served in the American military. Inasmuch as they did so, however, as long term citizens of a democratic society, their ethnic identity is subsumed within the general story and is recalled primarily within their own communities, just as are other ethnic veterans. The number of Jews in the Soviet armed forces was probably of comparable number, although exact figures are lacking. There is apparently no need to emphasize their Jewish identity in their respective countries save to point out to ignorant individuals that inherited prejudices are out of place and contribute nothing positive to the society at large.

In Greece, Jews were part of a democratic society whose constitution recognized Orthodox Christianity as the official religion of the state. Hence some Jews, for this and other reasons peculiar to their complicated history in the modern Greek kingdom, felt the need to emphasize their Jewish participation, especially in light of the conquest of Greece by the most anti-Jewish regime in history. Many, however, chose to obscure their Jewish origins under the guise of false names and papers.

The governments of Greece since the Revolution (1820–30) eschewed any anti Jewish prejudice.[10] The Church too restricted its anti-Judaism to a repetition of the theological and popular antipathy of its ancestral texts. It did not promote a policy of anti-Judaism comparable to that espoused and propagated by the leadership of the Catholic Church as part of its battle with modernity. The survival of medieval superstition and ignorance among Greek clergy (updated by attacks on Communists and Jews) was counterbalanced by the nobility of the Orthodox Church in Greece and elsewhere in its wartime attitude toward Jews.

Some 6 million Jews were killed in various ways that redefined the evils which an amoral technology could implement. But World War II was responsible for the deaths of about 50 million people, and many of these had national armies to defend them at some time during the war. Jews, however, have prominently raised the moral question of the killing of non-combatants and have turned this question into an intellectual discourse, supported by a plethora of bibliography and continued discussion.[11] Hence, war can no longer be treated as it traditionally has been, ignoring the vicissitudes of the civilian population. The moral question has entered the discourse of modernity and even postmodernity. To maintain an historical balance then, the response of the conquered peoples, and especially the Jews, should not be absent from the historiography of the war. My purpose in the following pages is to shed light on the fate of one Jewry and its contribution to the fight against evil in a homeland that welcomed Jews to fight both during its defense and during its resistance.

This case study may supply data for a reevaluation of subconscious elements that permeate western societies in the centuries since their emergence as Christian and Islamic. It may serve too as an example for the broader study of European and even Islamic societies in the period prior to World War II. At the least it will show that emancipated Jews can fight as well as any other citizens. Moreover, it will show that Jews can utilize well-developed skills in areas important to modern life and society to contribute services that the brave but uneducated ubiquitous foot soldier cannot.

ACKNOWLEDGEMENT

Research for this book was supported by the Center for Advanced Holocaust Studies while I was a Miles Lerman Center Fellow at the United States Holocaust Museum. Special thanks are due to the Charles Phelps Taft Memorial Fund at the University of Cincinnati for its continued support of my research on Greek Jewry. Photographs courtesy of the Jewish Museum of Greece and the family of Yaakov Arar.

NOTES

1. Michael Molho, *In Memoriam* (Salonika, 1948).
2. See my *Agony of Greek Jewry during World War II* (forthcoming).
3. See Michael Matsas, *Illusion of Safety* (New York, 1997).
4. Theodoros Kolokotronis, Συντομος Πραγματεια περι του Ισραηλιτικου Στρατου κατα την Αρχαιοτητα Κερκυρα, 1876), and summary in Χρονικα τομος κστ, αρ. 187 (Σεπτ-Οκτο, 2003), pp. 15–16.
5. See, for example, Benjamin Tudela's comments on Constantinople in my *Jews of Byzantium, 1204–1453* (Tuscaloosa, AL, 1985, repr. New York, 2000), appendix I, although there he notes western attitudes towards the Byzantines of the capital.
6. Islamic Spain was somewhat of an exception. Hisdai ibn Shaprut was able to hint at retaliation for the persecution of Jews during the tenth century by alluding to the Judaized king-

dom of Khazaria in his negotiations with the Byzantine rulers, and Samuel ibn Nagrela led Muslim armies into battle at the beginning of the eleventh century singing the war songs that he composed.

7. One exception is the Greek writer Yianni Berati (1904–68) who extols the heroism of the Jewish soldiers in Albania in his book *To Platy Potami* (The Wide River) (Athens, 1965) See Albert Nar's entry on Modern Greek Literature, in *Encyclopedia Judaica, Decennial Volume*, 1983–92 (Jerusalem, 1994), pp. 168f.

8. Czar Nicholas I instituted a policy of forced military service among Russian Jewry that resembled, *mutatis mutandis*, the Ottoman devşirme tax on Balkan Christians, shortly after the destruction of the Janissary Corps by their sultan. The USSR opened the door to military careers among the Jews of Russia, especially during and after World War II.

9. With the exception of course of Israel, where the military story is recognized as the corollary to the destruction on the one hand and as part of the nation-building process on the other. The former constitutes an integral part of the mission of Yad Vashem, the state-sponsored official agency for the preservation of the Holocaust and Jewish resistance. The latter is pursued in the history departments of Israeli universities; it is notably absent in the Jewish Studies curricula of the diaspora.

10. I exclude from discussion here the complicated competition in Salonika during the inter-war period and which I have analyzed elsewhere. See Ch. 2 and my forthcoming *Agony of Greek Jewry during World War II*.

11. This literature parallels the profusion of books and films about World War II with their stress on fighting. A futue sociologist of knowledge may help to clarify the importance of these two complimentary investigations of the war and the respective attitudes of each toward the other. There appears to be, aside from the animosity toward Jews evident among many intellectuals, an antipathy toward the growing library and the rhetoric of the Holocaust. It has even stimulated an internal debate among Jews, occasionally acrimonious, that has psychological overtones as much nationalistic as individualistic.

Introduction

The tragedy of the Jewish communities in Greece during World War II is starkly reflected in the numbers. In a country divided among Germany, Bulgaria and Italy there was a Jewish population estimated at 75,000–80,000, by far the largest percentage numbering about 55,000 in German-occupied Salonika. By Autumn 1944 only some 10,000 survived in Greece and perhaps another 2,000–3,000 returned from the camps during the summer of 1945.[1] In the period since the war, the number of Jews has shrunk to perhaps 5,000 and the viable communities to less than half a dozen. Perhaps a handful of communities flicker on with their aging populations; the latter most likely will be abandoned within another generation or be reduced to living museums to which a far-flung nostalgic diaspora will continue to make pilgrimage.

But on the eve of World War II there was a strong and robust generation of Jewish youth in Salonika busily becoming Hellenized after nearly a generation of exposure to Greek nationalism and the recent pressures of the regime of Ioannis Metaxas to learn the national language. The first generation of Greek control was rife with ethnic tensions, in particular between the Anatolian refugees and the Salonika community. A decade after the 1922 Katastrophe in Asia Minor, riots in Salonika stimulated a mass emigration of poorer Jews to Palestine. At the same time there was an exodus of the wealthier merchants to Paris and the West. The Metaxas coup of 1936 was aimed at resolving the broader social divide within Greece, yet its xenophobic fallout affected the Jews in its wake. Internally he outlawed the EEE whose violence against Jews was subject to Nazi and fascist influence. The regime also supported the new western Rabbi Zvi Koretz and maintained proper relations with the Jewish community. At the same time foreign language newspapers were closed (including several Jewish newspapers in Salonika) and anti-regime leftists were harassed while communists were outmaneuvered. Many of them recanted through signed confessions which led to their expulsion from the party; the stalwarts were imprisoned or exiled to Greek islands.

Many younger Jews continued their integration into the broader Greek society. They mastered Greek in the high schools, served in the army or went to university, and began to build lives within their local Jewish communities. When war broke out in the wake of the Italian invasion on October 28, 1940, some 13,000 Jews – veterans, volunteers and recruits – swelled the ranks and lower officer corps that drove the invaders back into the mountains of Albania where the Greeks held them at bay for nearly five months.

Jewish soldiers contributed to this victory in several ways. Colonel Mordechai Frizis, a career officer, became a national hero in the wake of his leadership in the successful counterattack, which turned the Italian flank. He was killed leading his men, machine-gunned by an Italian plane, along with four Jews from Larissa who had rallied to his horse. Frizis became a national symbol for the Metaxas propaganda; he was the highest-ranking officer to die on the battlefield. The other national hero of that war was a Greek infantryman, one of the many who set a new record for the longest bayonet charge (200 yards) against an entrenched enemy armed with machine-guns. The Greek infantry amazed the Italians who fretfully looked to the snow covered ridges and watched the Greeks continually outflank them. Jews also served in the air force and the navy.

But perhaps it was the quartermaster corps where Jews contributed most. Supplies came throughout the hard winter, carried on the backs of peasant women since honored for their heroic efforts; especially appreciated were the thousands of socks and sweaters knitted throughout Greece for soldiers fighting in sub-zero temperatures. Hot food and ammunition sustained the war effort. More important was the corps of Jewish doctors who refused to amputate frostbitten limbs as was the common recourse of their non-Jewish colleagues. The story of those six months still remains to be written, although numerous memoirs abound.[2]

Mussolini's overconfidence in his army and disdain for the Greeks coupled with poor preparation and inadequate logistics led him from defeat to defeat. Worried that British assistance to Greece would threaten his southern flank and thus jeopardize his planned invasion of the Soviet Union, Hitler decided to remove that threat by sending German troops to help his beleaguered ally to defeat the Greeks and subsequenty to drive out the British.[3] Hitler's decision sealed the fate of the Balkans for the next three and a half years during which time both the Jews and the non-Jews of the occupied countries suffered terribly. The vast majority of Jews were either deported to death camps or executed as hostages for acts of sabotage; non-Jews in their thousands were shot in reprisal or burned in their churches by punishment squads carrying out what was euphemistically called 'ethnic cleansing'. All of Greece suffered both dearth and death during the occupation, and in its wake the suffering was to continue through the long civil war whose roots it had nurtured.[4]

But the occupation did not start that way. In his May 4 1941 speech Hitler gave praise to the brave warriors of Greece. The Germans respected those who had held the Rupel Pass against their finest who today lie buried at the Bulgarian border that most failed to cross, and those who defended Crete where Hitler's elite paratroop corps was decimated. He announced that he would not take any of the Greek soldiers as prisoners of war; rather they should return home. He hoped that they would join his New Order since Greeks were the ancestors of the European Aryans from whose seed Hitler planned to repopulate his postwar realm. Among these valiant warriors was a myriad of Jewish soldiers. They too slogged home along with thousands of other veterans. Meanwhile, the national Greek government evacuated via Crete to Cairo.[5]

Though the Greek generals in Albania surrendered, nonetheless many of the common Greek soldiers along with a few of the remnants of the Serbian forces and escaped imperial POWs refused to surrender. Some officers and their men also stayed in the mountains where they joined with other Greeks (especially Cretans) and BEF troops, including a number of Palestinian Jews, to form the nuclei of resistance bands. They continued their resistance in haphazard fashion until the Greek Communist movement, neutral until the German attack on the Soviet Union in June 1941, called for national resistance and began to infiltrate, then organize, a serious partisan movement in the mountains. But this was in the future.

JEWS AND THE RESISTANCE

The Jewish participation in the Greek resistance movement can only be partially reconstructed from available sources and memoirs. Most Jews did not identify themselves as Jews, and many served in various facets of the resistance under assumed names. Hence their contribution was as Greeks, and so their identity as Jews generally went unrecorded in the official documents of the Resistance and the memoirs of many of its participants. Joseph Matsas, a veteran of the mountains, devoted his postwar years in Ioannina to a scholarly investigation of the Greek Jewish experience and to a roll call of Jewish fighters in the resistance.[6] His research was still unpublished at his death, but he succeeded in presenting some of it once the political climate in Greece became favorable to a reevaluation of the resistance during the war period. He estimated there were about 650 Jewish fighters (out of a total of some 30,000 *andartes*).

Matsas's preliminary research organized a discussion that had been carried on in muted tones since the war. Among the many Jews who immigrated into Israel in the postwar years were many that had participated in the *andartiko* [the fighting resistance]. A number of their memoirs and interviews shed light on Jewish activities. In addition to his estimate there should also be added those Greek Jews whom Matsas did not identify by name as well as foreign Jews from Austria, Yugoslavia, Bulgaria, even Poland, and Palestine. Among the latter were Salonikans in the BEF who were trapped in Greece following the British retreat. Therefore a figure closer to 1,000 Jews does not seem exaggerated, i.e. a little over 3 per cent, which was significantly higher than the percentage of Jews in the general population.[7] On the other hand, well over 12,000 Jews had been called up or were already serving in the Greek forces during the war. As Michael Matsas, Joseph's cousin and the most recent chronicler of Greek Jews during the war, has argued: had they known of Hitler's intentions there would have been a much larger number of Jewish fighters.[8]

But the Jewish role in the resistance cannot be restricted to those who fought. Many served in logistics, as recruiters, and as interpreters; several of the latter are listed on Christopher Woodhouse's pay roster.[9] Others contributed technical skills such as Josif Kohen in Crete, who operated as a printer for a few weeks.[10] Many in Athens were in contact with the urban cadres of EAM and functioning on the political level as well as gathering intelligence. Some acted in their capacity as lawyers and teachers and interacted with Greek politicians during the occupation (see Chapter 6). And finally there were those who fought in Greek units with the British in North Africa. Palestinian Jews worked with ELAS in establishing an escape route across the Aegean, while the Jewish Agency for Palestine made available to the Greek Resistance both money and needed supplies (see Chapter 3).

Moreover, many of the thousands of Jews who took refuge in the mountains had secondary and university level education as well as commercial and professional skills. Some of these individuals were instrumental in the development of the revolutionary society that EAM–ELAS created to bring modernization to the hitherto ignored Greek mountain communities. Many of the thousands of females who fled to the mountains served as nurses, some even attaining a reputation that became legendary.[11] Once their stories are collected and categorized, a clearer picture of the Jewish role in the resistance will be available to broaden our understanding of the mechanics of the movement during World War II.

Contrary to these political and military considerations, the collective memory of the Jews in the resistance (even today a touchy subject at best among those Jews in positions of authority) is rather low key. Younger Jews and those outside Greece opt for a more public study of this experience, yet few would research it. Thus many of the stories of heroism among Greek Jewry, which permeate the memoirs of survivors, resonate in the Greek discourse of 'freedom or death.' And many Jews did die in the mountains (and in the cities) during 1943 and 1944 to prove their right to Greek citizenship. Unfortunately, the postwar governments of Greece chose to persecute those who were in the mountains, and some Jews among them suffered accordingly. This experience accounts somewhat for the public reticence to pursue the subject.

The following stories will emphasize those Jews in the resistance who effected some kind of leadership role, not at the highest political levels, but on the field of battle or in the streets and offices of the urban centers. We shall find men and women whose stories are still untold or lie buried in obscure publications or in archival depositions. Many of the names listed in Appendices I and II have been harvested from family members or from aging *andartes*. It is my hope that, as these stories become better known, additional memories will surface so that a more balanced picture of the heroism of Greece in general and its Jews in particular will become an integral part of the wartime experience.

The pleasant task remains to thank all those who agreed to be interviewed, both the *andartes* and their relatives. To them and to the memory of their destroyed families this book is dedicated.

NOTES

1. My definition of Greece includes those areas added to the state after World War II, i.e. Corfu (briefly), Rhodes, and Cos, which had been under Italian control during the inter-war years. The aggregate number of Jews on these islands was about 4,000.

2. A philhellenic panegyric worth reading for its contemporary impact is Compton Mackenzie's *Wind of Freedom. The History of the Invasion of Greece by the Axis Powers 1940–1941* (London, 1943).

3. British philhellenism was still strong after a century of involvement in Greek affairs, and there was the strategic perspective ranging from Churchill's memory of Gallipoli and Salonika as well as the target of Romanian oil fields upon which Hitler relied.

4. The best book on the war to date is Mark Mazower, *Inside Hitler's Greece. The Experience of Occupation, 1941–1944* (New Haven and London, 1993).

5. Minos Levi of the Bank of Greece, who accompanied the king through the mountains, oversaw the safe transfer of the Greek gold reserves to Egypt whence they were removed to South Africa for the duration of the war.

6. Cf. My 'Joseph Matsas and the Greek Resistance,' *JHD* 17 (1991), pp. 49–53, and Joseph Matsas, 'The Participation of the Greek Jews in the National Resistance, 1940–1944,' ibid., pp. 55–68.

7. Even this estimate may be low. The report of an escaped Palestinian Jewish POW who fought with the resistance until late August 1943 estimates (somewhat exaggerated at this date) some 40,000 –50,000 in the resistance of whom about 3,000 were Jews, mostly Salonikans who escaped during the deportations (CZA S25 / 7852). For the story of the Bulgarian Jewish intellectual Saul Mezan who was rescued in a resistance-organized jailbreak from Ioannina and probably died fighting with a mixed band in Albania, see B. Arditi's report in *Ozar Yehudei Sepharad* 4 (1961), pp. 168f. (in Hebrew). Yosef Ben (*Greek Jewry in the Holocaust and the Resistance 1941–1944* (Tel Aviv, 1985), Ch. 8 (in Hebrew)) estimates a minimum of 800 but more likly as many as 1,000 of whom perhaps 300 died in battle (p. 125). The question for the researcher is how to define someone in the resistance. Should the definition be restricted to fighters alone? Should it include those who lived in the mountains as opposed to the reserves who were drafted from the villages for a particular mission? And if so, what was the relative strength of men at arms in 1942, 1943 and 1944? How many of those in the mountains were Greeks? How many Italians, Germans, Russians and other draftees or prisoners in the German forces, or Bulgarians and others fought with the Greek resistance forces at various times, especially towards the end of occupation. These questions have yet to be resolved, and various estimates will be brought below that will change the Jewish percentages accordingly. Estimates of the total number in the *andartiko* widely differ from 30,000 fighters to some 200,000 (including reserves).

8. In his *Illusion of Safety* (New York, 1997).

9. Liddell Hart Centre for Military Archives at King's College London contains the wartime reports of Edmund Myers and Christopher Woodhouse, the two major BLOs in Greece. Among the latter are the 'Nominal Rolls Force 133' dated August 1944 (Woodhouse III / 4–5) which include, among the list of 47 honorary commissions, the names of Jack Benveniste (joined AMM September 28, 1943) and Samuel Allalouf (joined November 10, 1943); and among the 50 non-commissioned those of John Besas (joined June 1, 1943 and Maurice Cazes (joined October 9, 1943). In an interview with the author, the Honourable Christopher Woodhouse (formerly an MP) could not recall meeting any Jews during his service in the Greek mountains. It is unlikely that those using their Jewish names or Christian aliases would have brought the issue to his attention. On the other hand, Michael Ward (*Greek Assignments. SOE 1943–1948 UNSCOB* (Athens, 1992), pp. 75f.) notes two Jewish sisters who escaped from Salonika and made their way to HQ Neraïda where they sought sanctuary; others, he notes, served as interpreters (see Appendix I).

10. As Judith Humphrey informed me based on Kohen's Yad Vashem testimony of 1967. Two Jewish girls apparently served as couriers in Chania.

11. Cf. Haim Politis in Miriam Novitch, *Passage des barbares* (Paris, 1967; 2nd edn Kibbutz Lohame Haghettaoth, 1982), and Afterword in this volume for one such story.

GREECE

Scale of Miles

50 40 30 20 10 0   50   100

Chief Railways
Chief Roads

Source: Compton Mackenzie, *Wind of Freedom: The Story of the Invasion of Greece by the Axis Powers 1940–1941* (London, 1943).

1

'To the Mountains'

Sta vouna (to the mountains) has been the traditional Greek response to lowland oppression, whether by urban Greek governments or by the Roman and Ottoman conquerors who ruled Greece for two millennia. And indeed the mountains have always remained free save for occasional punitive or tax collecting raids by the aforementioned occupying authorities . But they never stayed, and, besides, the mountain folk were always sure they would go away eventually. This was the case in Greece from 1941–1944. In a romanticized account based on his uncle's (Aron Yerushalmi) wartime memoirs set during the war, Leon Uris referred to the hills as being 'angry.'[1]

The hills, however, were not angry. Rather they were poor and neglected; then they were poor and filled with internecine fighting; then they were poor and subject to German 'cleansing raids' against *andartes*; then they were poor and began to organize. For nigh on a year the villages experienced collectivization enforced by ELAS or introduced by Jewish agronomy students.[2] They learned popular democracy through the ELAS People's Courts and its rough justice; and they also received education and medical treatment from the many educated refugees in the mountains. When the Germans left, the mountains were still poor, and they were to become poorer still, even devastated, during the subsequent civil war in Greece. World War II was the watershed of modernity for the mountains of Greece; today they are somewhat less poor due to the European Union and less populous due to the siren call of the city and diaspora.

It was to the freedom of the mountains that escaped POWs fled, where demoralized soldiers reverted to the klephtic tradition reminiscent of the biblical David and Yiphtah (Jephthah). A tradition that has become the classic theme of Crete, the exploits of its *kapetans* recounted by that island's great novelists Nikos Kazantzakis in *Freedom Or Death* and Pandelis Prevelakis in *The Cretan*. Yet the *klephts* (literally 'robbers') had become the folk heroes of Greeks under Ottoman occupation.[3] The renascent *klephts*, some outright bandits, were eventually controlled by ELAS once it had stamped its authority in the mountains. It then went even further and absorbed or destroyed all independent bands or rivals organized by the British (e.g. Brigadier Eddy [Edmund Myers] and other BLOs) except for EDES, which was restricted to western Greece. Since the Jewish military story in the mountains was primarily in the area controlled by ELAS, our story takes place primarily in the regions of Mount Olympus and Mount Pelion, Grevená, Paikon, and in the Naousa/Edessa region, i.e. northern and central Greece, and the Euboea (Evvoia) Sanctuary.[4]

Resistance in Greece continued in the wake of the formal surrender of the Greek forces in 1941: the Germans invaded the north in April, then overran the south in May, and finally conquered Crete at the beginning of June. The first members of the resistance were demobilized soldiers who wanted to continue the fight rather than walk hungry and barefoot for 500 to 1,000 kilometers to the uncertain future of their occupied homes. It was not, after all, until the beginning of May that Greek POWs were released by the Axis in the wake of Hitler's May 4th speech. Among the first Jews to go to the mountains was Elias Nissim from Salonika, one of the defenders of the Rupel Fort in Thrace. He was wounded in 1944 fighting in the area of Grevena and died of his wounds in the Pentalofos hospital.[5]

Those Jews who had become Communists, mostly from the poorer working classes (e.g. tobacco workers) of Salonika, had been drawn to the movement during the 1936 strikes.[6] They answered the Communist call to support Greece (albeit the government was still identified by them as 'monarcho-fascist') in 1940 against Italian Fascism; how much the worse was the conquest by German National Socialists in 1941 and its subsequent invasion of the USSR. Yitzhak Mosheh, a young tobacco worker from the Baron Hirsch quarter in Salonika, was drafted into the Greek army in March 1940 and served in Salonika, Verroia, and Naousa before being sent to the Albanian front. After the surrender, he joined ELAS in Salonika and escaped to Naousa. He recalls only 10–12 *andartes* in his band at the beginning, and some 200 by the summer.[7] In the beginning they stole food from the fields but by spring they were raiding German silos for distribution to the farmers. In addition to constant sabotage, destruction of bridges and roads, guarding food sources from German raids, he was also the political advisor for a platoon and later for a company.[8] Yitzhak Moshe's story, the story of *Kapetan* Kitsos, will be told in more detail in the following chapter.

Five members of the Bourla family fought under *Kapetan* Kitsos. Mosheh Bourla was active in the Communist movement and recruited a number of young Jews to the resistance. His good friend, an Orthodox Greek who happened to serve with the Salonika police, warned him to go to the mountains towards the end of May 1943. A day or so later the same policeman heard that the Germans intended to deport the neighborhood near the Great Synagogue (one of the last remaining in the center of the city). He hurried to mark the home of the Bourla family so that the Germans and the Greek police would pass it by. The following day he smuggled the family out of the city in a furniture truck. Bourla's two sisters (both nurses), Yolanda and Dora, were soon fighting in Vermion; the latter earned the nickname Tarzan for her exploits. His father Leon also fought in Vermion, while his mother Esther was hidden with a family in Naousa. His younger brother Solomon (Charles) was killed in September 1944 in a dramatic firefight near Verroia after killing several Germans. Mosheh Bourlas fought through to the end of the war. His subsequent vicissitudes belong to the persecution of Communist *andartes* during the civil war.[9]

The Bourlas was not the only family where everyone (save the mother) fought in the resistance. The recent memoir of Frederic Kakis identifies another, one unknown to the literature.[10] His father Emil, a decorated World War I explosives expert and a polyglot, was killed by the Germans, aged 52, while on a mission with the *andartes*. His older brother Zach was a captain with ELAS on Mount Pelion; he later trained junior officers in Arta. His sister Carmen was a recruiter for ELAS on Mount Pelion. Albert and Frederic were active members of EPON on Skiathos. It was due to their mother's skill and fluency in German as well as independent spirit that the orphans survived first in Salonika, where the family resettled after leaving Bulgarian-occupied Drama, and later in Skiathos. His future brother-in-law served with ELAN, the only Jew so far identified. It is clear from these two families that a determination to resist the occupier and to live where it would be difficult to reach was the decisive factor in their survival.

One more family supplied a number of members to the resistance. In subsequent chapters we shall meet the Noah family whose sons were active in the Albanian war in various branches of the military. Several of the Noah brothers continued in both the mountain and the urban Resistance.

Joseph Matsas was one of over a hundred young Salonikan Jews recruited by Markos Vafiades and led into the hills. Some of them later returned home to accompany their parents into what they thought was exile in Poland. Since he had combat experience in Albania, Matsas was assigned to a group of 40 fighters, 10 of whom were Jews. The solidarity evidenced by the KKE for the Jewish working and student class, forged during the early inter-war years, continued throughout the occupation period; however, only a minority of Jews who went to the mountains was sympathetic to communism. More were socialists who accepted the broader and public program of EAM for reforming Greek society. Even more were apolitical; they came out of desperation, as an escape from persecution and deportation. These, like their many compatriots, constituted the overwhelming majority of the Jews in the mountains, both those in the resistance and those in hiding. They filled the lower level officer and non-commissioned ranks of ELAS whose upper ranks were drawn by General Sarafis from Venizelist (republican) officers who had been retired during the Metaxas (monarchist) regime. Their educational and linguistic skills, as well as their organizing ability, allowed the Jews to complement the infrastructure of the resistance army of ELAS as they had already done so in the Greek regiments of the Albanian campaign.

David Aharon of Salonika, under the *nom de guerre* 'Keravnos', was recruited among a group of 45 Jews who joined ELAS, and claims a total of 450 Salonikan Jews in the mountains with ELAS, including 2 youths. One was a runner called Mosheh; the other, Carlo, was captured and tortured by the Germans. Aharon became an officer and was in charge of the weapon stores in his area. He recalled his first encounter with the Germans when an attack force of 35 attempted to surround his village. He and two other *andartes* (it later turned out they were also Jews) went out and captured two Germans while the rest fled. 'It became clear to us after they fled that the devil was not so terrible.' On another occasion, his commander (a general, as the leader of 1,500 *andartes* was called) fell off his horse and Keravnos saved him, whereupon he was assigned on the spot as his aide. Keravnos was also assigned to act as a liaison between headquarters and the British planes that flew in supplies for the *andartes*.[11]

Mosheh Segora of Salonika, whose *nom de guerre* was 'Toto', headed a platoon of EPON, under the command of Aris Velouhiotis, one of the founding leaders of ELAS, which occasionally fought German soldiers and right wing resistance forces.[12] At first his unit fought in the region of Ioannina; he also took part in the destruction of the Pindos Bridge and participated in rail sabotage with the Allied Mission. During the German retreat in autumn 1944, his unit engaged 'rightist' partisans near Kilkis. The units interestingly were mixed: his unit included Italians who had defected to ELAS, while their opponents included German soldiers. On another occasion, when the enemy surrendered, the ELASites sent their Italians to collect the weapons. They were massacred. The ELASites attacked, killing most of the enemy; the handful that surrendered was executed in revenge. He avers his unit was the first to enter liberated Salonika.

The Negrin clan of Trikala and Karditsa contributed several *andartes* of note. Benjamin Negrin, whose *nom de guerre* was 'Maios', rose to command a platoon in ELAS Regiment 1/38. He was severely wounded leading a successful attack against entrenched German forces in April 1944. After treatment in an *andartiko* hospital, he returned to perform actions that became legendary. Such wartime exertions weakened him so much that he succumbed to an illness in late 1945.[13] Albert Negrin traveled through the villages of Thessaly as a recruiter for ELAS. In March 1944, he was near Trikala, and decided to visit his family to celebrate the Passover holiday. He was caught up in the massive German arrests and spent the remainder of the war in Nazi concentration camps.[14]

The many stories of Jewish *andartes* hitherto made available add to our knowledge of the resistance, but not necessarily to our understanding, other than to note that Jews were in the mountains. The reason for this lies in the personal narrative of the accounts and reflects the limited awareness that the participants had of the entire picture. This indeed is what makes them so valuable for an understanding of the rank and file experience during the occupation. Moreover, after the war they continued to remember their own participation, which they occasionally shared with *synagonistes* but otherwise kept a low profile for a number of reasons. First was government pressure on former *andartes*, including imprisonment. Second was the reticence of the Jewish leadership, especially in the north where the political situation was hostile to the Left. And third was the communal emphasis on the sufferings and loss of the majority of Jewish victims in Auschwitz and Treblinka. Also, only one scholar emerged out of the Jewish fighting resistance: Joseph Matsas who published but a fraction of the materials he collected. All these factors, and other considerations, contributed to the silence.

The postwar scholarly study of the Greek resistance falls into three categories:

1. The Left's treatment of the Communist story mostly told by expatriate Greeks. There are also a number of memoirs by Communist leaders, in particular Markos Vafiades.[15] The important history of ELAS by General Stephanos Sarafis sets one frame for the military actions.

2. Accounts by BLOs of their activities and subsequent studies based on British archival material have appeared since the war and continue to dominate public perception of the period.[16] There is happily an over-abundance of local, albeit undigested, data thanks to the efficiency of the Greek men and women of the resistance who funneled masses of information to the Allies.[17] The American reports of the Allied Mission lie mostly in manuscript and are unknown except to the participants and literally a handful of scholars. Now that the OSS files have been declassified (in 2000) more studies of the Greek-American contribution to the war in Greece should begin to appear.

3. Recent scholarship has exploited the captured records of the Italian and German armies and diplomatic reports sent from the occupation zones.[18] Lately the Bulgarian zones have seen more scholarly study; this material has been supplemented by postwar Greek trials of collaborators.[19]

The Jewish anecdotes and memoirs, then, need not float in limbo. There exists a structure within which to place them preparatory to their evaluation as contributions to the war effort. That is a larger project, however, than the one that constitutes this book, since it is part of the story of the revolution in the mountains which still has yet to be written. To date no researcher has integrated the Jewish story into any aspect of the general Greek experience during the war.[20] Such an approach does not serve well the Jews of Greece. Those who fought or went to serve with the *andartiko* did so as Greeks. Those who sought refuge did so, some as Greeks, but most as Jews who were being hunted by the Nazis to fuel their death factories, although too few Jews were aware of the tragic fate awaiting them. As *Kapetan* Kitsos told me, 'All my men knew I was a Jew, and I was proud to let it be known that a Jew was fighting for Greece.' He was responding to a long tradition of denigration of the Jews by certain segments of the Greek military (both regular and irregular). But then Greece was not alone in evidencing this attitude; most of the European nationalist militaries were even more blatant if not overtly anti-Semitic, and this attitude carried over into the many partisan movements in Europe during the war.[21]

The question facing us is how then to approach the framing of our material. Many anthologies of the resistance have usually just assembled them for the reader and so provide a collection of material for future researchers.[22] The state of research to date is not yet sufficiently developed to write the complete history of Jewish participation, which would contribute another perspective to the wartime experience in Greece. Since the material is mostly unknown save for a handful of studies that have appeared in various languages, even this preliminary study in English is a desideratum that is long overdue. In the following chapters, which should be considered as a contribution to that history, I shall attempt to contextualize the stories that have been collected and integrate them into the broader rhythm of the mountains during the three and a half years of the occupation.

We can begin by identifying five stages of Jewish participation in the fighting resistance during the occupation. Some of these stages coincide with the general recruitment of the Greek rural population to the *andartiko*:

1. Those Jews who refused to surrender and continued to fight in the mountains in the late spring and summer of 1941 – this stage included some remnants of the BEF and scattered units of the Serbian and Greek armies. This period witnessed the appearance of numerous bands of *klephtes*, some of whom were patterned on the earlier tradition of mountain robbers.
2. Those Jews who escaped the forced labor from the end of summer 1942 and were absorbed into various bands of *klephtes* and *andartes* (see Chapter 4). Others went to the mountains for ideological reasons (see Chapter 2).
3. Those recruited or aided by the KKE or EAM in the spring of 1943, primarily in Salonika, but also elsewhere in Greece. Also, Jews from families that escaped to the mountain villages were drafted into ELAS units.
4. Those who escaped Athens in the fall of 1943 and went to the mountains; they found an organized but still fledgling army (ELAS) in the field. Many of these were of military age and were drafted if they did not volunteer.
5. Those who left the former Italian zone in the spring of 1944 during the deportations in time to fight against the retreating German forces.

The first stage really belongs to the epilogue of the Italo-German war and is treated elsewhere.[23] There we follow the actions and exploits of the Palestinian contingent in the BEF. More systematic research in the archives and memoirs of those participants may illuminate the subsequent role of the Palestinian Jews in the resistance both in occupied Yugoslavia and in Greece. The second stage blends into the third as we shall see during the course of the remaining chapters. The fourth and

fifth stages cover the last year of the war and those Jews who found an
organized resistance movement where they could integrate.

The third stage, which lasted for about six months from March
through August 1943, is most crucial for an understanding of the resistance. Among the many bands, some royalist, some republican, and the
majority socialist, three emerged to dominate the postwar historiography: EDES, EKKA and EAM–ELAS. The major organization, sub-
scribed to by most of the mainland and nearly all of the islands (save
Crete), was EAM–ELAS, whose complicated history has been obfuscated by the postwar politics of participants and many scholars. A central
command for ELAS was set up in mid-May 1943 that, facing a major
Italian sweep into the mountains of Central Greece, forced the movement to assemble the scattered *andartiko* bands in Macedonia and
Thessaly on the Pindos range. There it was able to forge a broader resistance identity among them, which enabled EAM–ELAS to continue its
revolution in the mountains and restrict (by force) the other organizations to Epirus and Thrace.[24] During the summer Brigadier Edmund
Myers succeeded in effecting a union – albeit temporary – between the
fledgling organizations of ELAS and EDES. During the same period the
American OSS began to organize its venture into the turbulent waters
of the Balkan resistance where it functioned subordinate to the British
Military Mission, now renamed the Allied Military Mission (AMM).[25]

These six months are perhaps the most difficult period for the study
of the involvement of Jews, since they witnessed the deportations from
Salonika, the great reservoir of Greek Jews. Few oral or written memoirs survive. The resistance in the mountains was only formally organized by summer 1943 during the period of the last deportations. The
last trainload of Salonikan Jews (the nineteenth such transport[26]) left on
the night of August 10/11 and arrived in Auschwitz on August 18. It
consisted of 1,800 Jews who had been selected for forced labor in late
March along with the last families in the city.[27]

A mass escape to the mountains, even by potential fighters let alone
the aged and the very young, was simply not feasible at this time – how
much the more so during the previous six months – since there was no
infrastructure there to absorb, let alone rescue, them. Not that anyone in
Greece – Jew or Gentile – thought in such terms of rescue or mass
recruitment![28] Those who did make it to the mountains had been individually recruited, usually by Christian or Communist family friends.
Most of the recorded stories of Jews cover the last year and a half of the
German occupation. This reality on the ground as well as that in the
available sources puts into better perspective the relationship between the

deportations from Salonika and the *andartiko*.[29] It illustrates the imbalance of the story we are uncovering. History, however, is based upon sources, and we should be constantly aware of the fragmentary nature of the written and oral sources that we have collected. It is also based upon chronology, and the latter is generally unforgiving to any emotional approach.

Dr Errikos Levi of Ioannina is a good example of our difficulty. A career officer in the Greek army, he served as a physician in an artillery division. During the occupation he acted as interpreter for the Germans. In 1943 he worked in Athens at the 15th military hospital and as medical officer in the Department of Public Safety. After the deportations from Salonika he returned to Ioannina with his family with the intention of joining Zervas and EDES. Along with Major Makrinioti of the Greek police and others he spied for Zervas, supplying vital information for EDES sabotage attempts. When he did go to the mountains to escape Italian suspicions, Zervas sent him back with the observation that he was more useful as a German-speaking spy than another addition to his well-staffed medical corps. He was captured in February 1944 and sent to Auschwitz with nearly the entire Jewish community of Ioannina, many of whose men he was able to save during their peregrinations over the next year. After the war he returned to the army and retired as a colonel, and was recognized finally for his resistance contributions in 1988.[30]

One of the few Jews to serve with EDES was his friend David Nahmias who was Zervas's personal guard. According to Raphael and Nina Nahmias, he only had to use his pistol three times. Later he was captured by ELAS and was about to be shot when an officer recognized his old friend and ordered him released. Nahmias was drafted by ELAS, a life-saving happenstance. However, it would later cost him his commission; he was demoted after the war and served as a sergeant major for nine years.[31]

Albert Preznalis is another such example. He had fled Bulgarian-occupied Serres in 1941 for Salonika and returned home only after the deportations began. A Greek Christian friend suggested that he join the *andartes*, so he went to a group which was active near the villages of Sevastia and Sohos. His responsibilities included the acquisition of supplies, which were usually obtained from the occupying forces. Later he participated in the fighting against Germans, Bulgarians, and collaborationist Greeks who comprised the complex reality of Thrace and Macedonia. His is a typical example of the memory of an *andartis*, it lacks context – even more so when the interviewer is not always aware of the right questions to ask in order to stimulate memory.[32]

Preznalis recalled a number of Greek Jews in his band, whose names were not recorded during our meeting, and, additionally, a Polish Jew named Jan (Jacob) Fuerst, who, in a subsequent interview with this author in London, recalled several engagements, especially against the German 999 units in Chalkidiki.[33] It was Fuerst's responsibility to entice them to desert to the Greeks and fight against the Nazis who had persecuted them. Some of the latter indeed joined the *andartes*; they refused, however, to fight against any German forces other than SS units, whom they hated and wished to see destroyed.[34] ELAS did not conceive of such a plan on its own since it had no prior knowledge of the composition of these units. Rather the Greeks were informed of the potential for recruiting these disaffected units by a German defector. Dr Manfred Messerschmidt of the Waldheim Commission recounted to me (November 1994) his interview with Falk Harnak, a Wehrmacht radio sergeant whose brother was accused of being a Russian spy and was subsequently shot by the Germans. Angered at this injustice, Harnak went to the Greek resistance (perhaps in the summer of 1943) and told them about the 999 battalions, explaining that they comprised political prisoners and 'socialists'. He advised the resistance to entice them to desert and to allow them to fight only against SS battalions.[35]

Jewish *andartes* from the north are somewhat harder to track amidst the chaos of Macedonia, a still unclarified story. The local ethnic groups, living a precarious existence – some since the nineteenth century and others since the massive Asia Minor immigration of the 1920s – were under constant pressure from Italians, Germans, Bulgarians, and Greeks to declare a political preference.[36] Jews were, as were other minority groups in Macedonia, understandably ambivalent about whom to support. Joseph Cohen from Florina, for example, contacted his teacher, Rabbi Bibas, and asked him to organize local Jewish youth for the resistance. Joseph was sure of his support since the rabbi sympathized with the Zionist Revisionists. He had taught his students, for example, the story of Jewish resistance at Tel Hai in Upper Galilee where Joseph Trumpeldor, co-founder of the Zion Mule Brigade and the Jewish Legion during World War I, died defending that outpost in northern Palestine in 1920. The rabbi responded, however, that the partisans were all Communists. Nevertheless Joseph took four lads with him, including his younger brother Pinhas, along with seven Christian boys. He recalled fighting in the mountains with ten Jews, among them four girls, from Bitola, Yugoslavia. He attests to the partisans[37] that fought with the *andartes*; indeed the border was easily penetrated and individuals as well as units fought throughout the Macedonian mountains during the occupation. Cohen claimed that the resistance saved 25 percent of the Jews of Florina and helped 90 of them to flee to the Italians in Kastoria.[38]

Many urban Jews also found their way to the *andartiko* throughout the occupation. Isaac Nehama of Athens (born 1927), for example, following discussions with his parents, fled to Thessaly after September 1943 and was directed to a monastery in the Pindos Mountains where he joined ELAS' First Regiment of Evzones. Isaac had learned Ladino at home and French at a Catholic primary school, and had attended the Greek gymnasium. He served as telephone operator and cipher clerk in the area of Trikala and Larissa and at least once participated in a sabotage operation against a German convoy during March 1944.[39]

Paul Noah, on the other hand, came from a family active during the war and the resistance. He moved to Athens from Salonika during the war and advised his parents to do the same and open a store there. One of his brothers was a sergeant at the Bulgarian front, a second was a skier in the Greek army in Albania; they later hid with Christians and subsequently disappeared under unknown circumstances that may have been connected with Allied intelligence. A third, Isidore, was a technical manager of an aircraft factory, while Paul served with the admiral corps in Athens. During the occupation he and his friends established a committee to raise funds and assist the Salonikan refugees; he was eventually saved by EAM. Isidore went to the mountains where he became an officer, and was responsible for blowing up bridges. He later assisted in the kidnap rescue of Rabbi Barzilai.[40]

Some light is shed on one of the Noah brothers and other facets of the resistance in the memoir of Salvatore Ben Yaish, which contains insights into Greek and German attitudes toward Jews. As a draftee with the rank of sergeant he was in charge of the communication center on the Bulgarian border. On October 26 1940 he was posted to Albania. He reports the following conversation that he had with his colonel on October 28 as the post was being bombed by the Italians:

> Colonel   'Jew, are you there?'
> Ben Yaish 'Yes.'
> Colonel   'What are you doing there?'
> Ben Yaish 'My duty.'
> Colonel   'Where are the others?'
> Ben Yaish 'In the shelter.'

This conversation netted him a promotion and a medal. He served for the next six months at the front before being captured. After six weeks as a POW, he escaped to join ELAS. He recalled the disastrous attack on a factory in Naousa that was under German control where ELAS suffered 50 percent losses trying to get food and water. Later Major Jones, a Greek-speaking BLO, parachuted into the ELAS camp near Previna. After learning that Ben Yaish was a Jew he convinced him to leave the Communist-controlled organization. So Ben Yaish and another Jew, Shlomo Shenka, escaped to Karditsa and then to Athens where they made their way through Greek and German roadblocks the day before the Italian surrender (September 9, 1943). Shaul Noah hid them in Athens. They then stayed with an airforce general, George Lembais, who was in contact with the British. Next they hid in a priest's house in Philadelphia, 15 kilometers from Athens, on orders from Archbishop Damaskinos. The Germans, according to Ben Yaish, executed the priest at the beginning of 1944 for helping Jews.[41]

The Jews of Volos contributed 71 fighters during the war while many others served in support units. Several died as *andartes*, including Iakov Savvas and Leon Sakis. The latter's brother, Moissis, was a leader of ETA in Thessaly.[42] Active in the rescue of the Jews of Volos were Ioakim, Bishop of Demetrias, who was informed by Helmut Scheffel, the German Consul in Volos, about the fate of the Jews if arrested. Such admissions by German officials are extremely rare and hence noteworthy. The mayor of Volos, Nicholas Saratsis; the Municipal Official, Zissis Mantidis; the police chief, Ilias Agdiniotis; and many other citizens facilitated the escape of the octogenarian Chief Rabbi Moses Pessah and some 600 local Jews and refugees.[43] Once in the mountains they came under the protection of EAM-ELAS.[44]

The fifth and last stage is represented by Armando Aaron from Kerkira (Corfu). During the deportation of June 1944, which stopped at Patras, Armando was waiting in line for further orders when he received permission from a Greek guard to stand to one side to talk with an old friend. Out of line when the column began to move, Armando was approached by Georges Mitzales (or Mitsiales), a young barber who offered to rescue him. Whether he had any foreknowledge of the fate that awaited Armando is not known, but it is likely that he offered to help him escape because he perceived Armando's arrest as unjust. Mitzales took him to the village of Komi where he joined ELAS, remaining with them for the final four months of the occupation. His duties included procurement of food and keeping accounts, and armed battle.[45] In the complicated arena of the Peloponnesus we also find Baruch Shibi, an Athens leader in EAM, during the latter stages of the war.[46]

We have already noted several reasons why the *andartiko* recruited among Jews, particularly in Salonika. The opening of the OSS archives in 2000 has revealed a report that may shed light on another facet of this recruitment that goes beyond the traditional Greek perspective. The report is not corroborated by other sources; however, for our purposes it provides a link that is otherwise even more tenuous. The report, dated October 26, 1942, notes that four Russian agents had entered Salonika and three more were in Piraeus. They had come from Bulgaria and Yugoslavia 'for the purpose of organising communist bands to resist the Axis along the pattern of the Partisans in Yugoslavia.'[47] The same report claims that Russian supplies were being smuggled into Greece. There were already Communist leaders in Greece who had before the war received training in the Soviet Union, and their loyalty to the Soviet regime was unquestioned; local Communists were of the same order.[48] Hence the question arises – and remains unanswered – whether there was a specific message from Moscow to the KKE regarding Jews.

During the first two years after the German invasion of their country, the Soviet attitude toward Jewish partisans in particular and to the Jews in general underwent a number of revisions. Even before the invasion the border with Germany was sufficiently porous for many Jews to escape into the Soviet Union, although for a large number this was but a temporary reprieve as they were later to be caught in the slaughter of the *Einsatzgruppen*. The growth of the Soviet partisan forces was slow due to the savagery of the Nazi advance and to Stalin's reluctance to allow autonomous armed units among the Soviet masses. The earliest partisans were not concerned, save a few leaders, for the dilemma of the Jews. They rejected Jewish volunteers and even aided in the killings, albeit from different motives than the Nazis. Hence even Jewish partisan units were at risk from Soviet partisans. The situation changed during the summer of 1942 at the urging of P. K. Ponomarenko, the Byelorussian First Secretary who headed the Central Staff of the Partisan Movement.[49] At Ponomarenko's urging and upon the advice of partisan leaders, Stalin redefined the partisan movement in the People's Commissariat of Defense Order No. 189, 'On the Tasks of the Partisan Movement,' dated September 5, 1942. It was now to be a 'people's war' that 'should include all honorable male and female citizens desiring liberation from the German yoke.' There is no reason to suspect that this order was not made known to

Communist partisans throughout Europe, and may even provide part of the rationale for the alleged visit to Greece noted in the OSS agent's report (despite any confirmation in KKE or Soviet sources).

Even if this suggestion does not prove to be a missing link in the emergence of an active Communist resistance in Greece, there is no doubt that the other factors we noted above contributed to the recruitment of Jews in Salonika.[50] Moreover, they were likely candidates: many of them had military experience; they were decidedly anti-Nazi; and they were being persecuted in both the city and the forced labor camps. Save for a few, however, the majority of military age Jews decided not to answer the call to the *andartiko* at the end of 1942 and the beginning of 1943. By spring 1943 when they did begin to join, it was too late for most of the potential recruits who had already decided to accompany their families into exile and had been deported to Auschwitz.

NOTES

1. Leon Uris, *The Angry Hills* (New York, 1955).
2. See Yad Vashem testimony of Max Varon of Kavalla [#03/2989] summarized in John O. Iatrides (ed.), *Greece in the 1940s. A Bibliographic Companion* (University Press of New England, 1981), pp. 85–86.
3. Among others see John Koliopoulos, *Brigands with a Cause: Brigandage and Irridentism in Modern Greece* (Oxford, 1987).
4. No one has suggested a figure higher than four Jews with EDES, and these were mostly physicians according to Michael Matsas. See his *Illusion of Safety* (New York, 1997), pp. 283f. for Dr Henry (Errikos) Levi (pp. 283f) and pp. 298ff. for Dr Michael Negrin. A more detailed memoir of Dr Henry (Errikos) Levi is in the Hebrew University of Jerusalem (hereafter HUJ). The Institute for Contemporary Jewry, Oral History Division, 146/18. There were others, however, as we shall see. ELAS units operated occasionally in the vicinity of Ioannina, and one included the Salonikan Mosheh Segora (below); see Matsas, *Illusion of Safety*, pp. 310f. for the adventures of several youths caught in the rivalry between EDES and ELAS.
5. Joseph Matsas, 'The Participation of the Greek Jews in the National Resistance, 1940–1944,' *JHD* 17 (1991), pp. 66f.
6. In 1919 many of the Jewish workers began to support the Socialist Federation of Labor organized by Abraham Benaroya; cf. Joshua Starr, 'The Socialist Federation of Saloniki,' *Jewish Social Studies* 7 (1945), pp. 323–36.
7. YVS 03/4542; he avers some 500 Jews with the *andartes* in his area by the end of April 1943. Many of them had combat experience in Albania, and they had left Salonika and other German occupied towns for the mountains during the previous winter. EAM organized support for their families through EPON.
8. ELAS had a tripartite leadership for each unit consisting of a military leader, a representative of EAM, and a *kapetan*. A section consisted of 3 leaders, a 6-man machine gun crew, and 6 skirmishers, i.e., 15 men; a platoon of 3 sections; a company of 3–4 platoons, a battalion of three-four companies, a regiment of 3–4 battalions. The whole army was eventually organized into at least seven divisions and a number of specialized Brigades (cf Stephanos Sarafis, *ELAS. Greek Resistance Army* (London, 1980), pp. 156 and 166f.). The army was structured to be 'light and mobile' with the emphasis on small guerrilla missions of sabotage and ambush.
9. Interview with author, spring 1996. An English version of his Greek memoir *Ellinas, evraios kai aristeros* (Skopelos, Greece, 2000 is forthcoming entitled *A Greek, A Jew And A Leftist* by Moisis Michail Bourlas.
10. *Legacy of Courage. A Holocaust Survival Story in Greece* (Bloomington, IN, 2003).

11. Yosef Ben, *Greek Jewry in the Holocaust and the Resistance 1941–1944* (Tel Aviv, 1985) p. 127 (in Hebrew).
12. EPON was the youth movement of ELAS; it undertook various assignments including fighting.
13. Matsas, *The Illusion of Safety*, pp. 294f., summarizing the account in 'Israelitiko Vima,' 2/15/46.
14. Interview with author. Negrin produced a video of his memoir, which he kindly supplied to me. Many of the Jewish males from Trikkala were drafted from the Auschwitz quarantine directly to labor camps and so never experienced the horror of that death camp. Indeed, he claims, they were unaware of the murder of their families until much later.
15. Markos Valiades, *Apomnimonevmata* (Athens, 1985). A critical reading of this literature is available by Hagen Fleischer, in John O. Iatrides (ed.), *Greece in the 1940s. A Bibliographic Companion* (Hanover, NH and London). See his *Im Kreutzschatten der Mächte: Griechenland 1941–1944*, 2 vols (Frankfurt am Main, 1986) and the updated Greek version *Stemma kai Swastika* (Athens, 1988).
16. A good summary of this material is by André Gerolymatos, *Guerrilla Warfare & Espionage in Greece 1940–1944* (New York, 1992). The SOE files located in Kew Gardens, London are now open to researchers and contain both the BLO reports and the oversight commentary.
17. Happily preserved if undigested during the war. Cf. Gerolymatos, *Guerrilla Warfare & Espionage*.
18. John Hondros, *Occupation and Resistance: The Greek Agony, 1941–44* (New York, 1983) summarized the German experience in studies. An early assessment based on interviews with German generals to supplement the printed material is Department of the Army CMH Pub 104–18, (written by Robert M. Kennedy), *German Antiguerrilla Operations in the Balkans (1941–1944)*(Washington, DC, 1954).
19. The reader is well served by reading the 'Note on Sources' in Mark Mazower, *Inside Hitler's Greece. The Experience of Occupation, 1941–1944* (New Haven and London, 1993) pp. 423–8.
20. Mazower, *Inside Hitler's Greece*, devoted a special chapter to the Jews as did Hondros, *Occupation and Resistance*. The latter was based primarily on the immediate postwar story compiled by Michael Molho and Joseph Nehama, *In Memoriam* (Salonika, 1948 and later editions).
21. See Preface. Prejudices, especially among an entrenched class, die hard. Greek and Turkish fighters in the Balkans used the terms 'coward' and 'Jew' interchangably as insults during the nineteenth century.
22. So Matsas in his *Illusion of Safety*, which contributes many new memoirs to the tradition of Jewish resistance in Greece.
23. Steven Bowman, *Agony of the Greek Jewry during World War II* (forthcoming).
24. See Mazower, *Inside Hitler's Greece*, pp. 298f. and *passim*. The Greek Communists subject to Soviet influence ultimately directed ELAS; the vast majority of the members or auxiliaries of ELAS, however, had no idea of this relationship. The British were to exploit the Communist connection to their purpose, while the Americans were ordered to remain strictly neutral on the political front and only prosecute the war against the German and Bulgarian occupying armies.
25. That story has only recently come to light and deserves more detailed study.
26. On the number of transports, see my *Agony of Greek Jewry*, Ch. 5.
27. Danuta Czech, *Auschwitz Chronicle 1939–1945. From the Archives of the Auschwitz Memorial and the German Federal Archives* (New York, 1997), p. 465. Of these, 271 young men were selected for admission into the camp and tattooed with numbers ranging from 136919 to 137189. The remaining men, women and children were gassed and the bodies cremated. In an interview with the author, Isaac Senior (#137135), affirmed that the young men from this transport were the first to be selected for forced labor in the ruins of the Warsaw ghetto having been transferred there in late September 1943. Among them were David Zvi (#137142) and his brother (#137141). A number of these slaves fought in the Warsaw revolt of August 1944. See Ch. 7.
28. During the first six months of the occupation some 5,000 Jews, it has been estimated, had left Salonika primarily for Athens in the Italian zone; but they left as individuals, and many returned to Salonika within a year. The Greek experience differed from the situation in Yugoslavia where Tito's partisans included an entourage of non-combatants and as well hosted peasants during sweeps by German troops; see Franklin Lindsay, *Beacons in the Night. With the OSS and Tito's Partisans in Wartime Yugoslavia* (Stanford, CA, 1993).
29. This perspective may answer the assumption of Michael Matsas, based on his experience and

those of the Jews in the former Italian zone, that all one had to do was get in a bus or a taxi and ride off to the mountains. It was not that easy in the environs of Salonika.

30. See Matsas, *Illusion of Safety*, pp. 283ff., and Levi's memoir in HUJ, Oral History Division.
31. See memoir in HUJ, Oral History Division, 146/19. It is not known whether other Jews served with EDES. Pyramoglou, Zervas's lieutenant, wrote to Marcel Yoel that he was of the opinion that there were some Jews who served under Christian aliases. His letter was in an archive that Yoel transferred to KIS in Athens during the 1950s. Its current location is unknown. Yoel interview with author, November 2002. Other former *andartes* that I interviewed suspected that there were no more than a dozen Jews, all with aliases, in EDES.
32. See his memoir in Miriam Novitch, *Passage des barbares*.
33. Interviews with Preznalis in 1972 and with Fuerst in 1988. The 999 units were *Strafbattalions*, punishment units that were made up from political and criminal prisoners of the state, some of whom volunteered for the military in order to get out of concentration camps. There were also 999 units on Zakynthos and Rhodes in 1944 doing guard duty. The differing fates of the Jews of those islands militate against a blanket absolution of such units in their wartime records.
34. Not all such attempts were successful of course. Theodore Hirschhorn, a Viennese Jew who had worked as a knitting technician for the Melissa mill in Salonika and was a member of EAM, escaped to the partisan controlled village of Ormylia in Chalkidike where he continued to assist both partisans and villagers. At the end of August 1944 the Germans left Ormylia. Hirschhorn volunteered to accompany an ELAS mission to induce the Germans in a fort at Porto Koufo (Sithonia) to surrender. He was captured and imprisoned in Pavlos Melas but released when the Germans left the city. (Letter of December 4, 1999 in author's files).
35. One of the objectives of the OSS 'Ulysses' mission to Pelion was to encourage German defections. Eventually the British, who ran the 'show' in Greece, curtailed this approach. The British policy passed on to the Americans was to accept only battalion strength surrender and it officially discouraged individual defections. The Americans understood this policy as an attempt to deny arms and manpower to ELAS.
36. Most recently discussed by John S. Kolioupolis, *Plundered Loyalties. World War II and Civil War in Greece West Macedonia* (New York, 1999).
37. The Yugoslavian term for their guerrillas and used interchangeably as partisans with *andartes* in the literature. Cohen estimated some 2,000 Jewish fighters, but did not specify how many of them were Greek or Yugoslavian. The Jews of Yugoslavian Macedonia were arrested by the Bulgarians in March 1943 and sent to Treblinka where all of them were killed. See Zhamila Kolonomos and Vera Veskovich-Vangeli, *The Jews in Macedonia During the Second World War (1941–1945)*, 2 vols (Skopje, 1986).
38. Material collected in March 1997 in Tel Aviv.
39. USHMM Photo Archives W/S #00; and interview with author August 2002.
40. See memoir in HUJ, Institute for Contemporary Jewry, Oral History Division, 25 (146), and Ch. 6.
41. HUJ, Oral History Division, 146/1.
42. *Epimelitia tou Andarti* – the Guerrilla Commissariat of ELAS; see Matsas, *Illusion of Safety*, pp. 221f., who brings other witnesses to this story.
43. Rafael Frizis, ed., *The Jewish Community of Volos. A brief historical overview* (Volos, 1985) is recognized as the official recollection of the Jewish community.
44. For the vicissitudes of the family of Victor Daskalakis, whose family owned the well known clothing store 'Les Frères Daskalakis' in Volos, see Vital Eliakim, *Souvenirs de jeunesse d'un juif salonicien* (n.p., 1997). He provides a description of conditions in Karpenissi during 1943 and 1944.
45. The story is told in varying detail by Mazower, *Inside Hitler's Greece*, p. 255; by Matsas, *Illusion of Safety*, pp. 291–4 from Aaron's letter to him; and from an oral interview at The United States Holocaust Memorial Museum, RG-50.443*003.
46. See his memoir in Novitch, *Le passage des barbares*, and below Ch. 6.
47. NARA, RG 210 Box 410 Folder 3; henceforth cited as NARA, RG/Box/Folder.
48. D. George Kousoulas, *Revolution and Defeat. The Story of the Greek Communist Party* (London, 1965), rather sharply emphasizes this point.
49. Kenneth Slepyan, 'The Soviet Partisan Movement and the Holocaust,' *Holocaust and Genocide Studies*, 14 (spring, 2000), pp. 1–27; our remarks follow pp. 10–11.
50. See Chs 3 and 5 for the attitudes of EAM.

Kapetan Kitsos: Freedom or Death

The sun manifests more slowly in the Greek summer. It rises languidly above Thrace, shining on the Chalkidiki peninsula that juts into the northern Aegean, and slowly warms the patch of garden homes stretching along the Thermaic Gulf east of the great graveyard of the Jews, whose denizens, accumulating since the sixteenth century, numbered in the hundreds of thousands. The light crawls west along Tsimiskes Street, whose stores await their proprietors, and soon reaches the stretch from Plateia Aristotelos to Plateia Eleutheria, where the Jews have begun to stir towards their many synagogues, hurriedly to offer praises to their God before opening the central markets to the hordes of nations who live within and about Salonika. By the time the light reaches the Baron Hirsch quarter it is tiring, as tired as the poor who inhabit this small compound near the railway, a slum swarming with life but hungry for work, a center for tobacco workers, seamstresses, servant girls, porters, fishermen, and other poverty-level occupations that earned little more than daily bread.

Salonika had changed greatly in the space of a generation. At the end of the nineteenth century the sea walls were torn down and replaced by a promenade; and tramlines were laid along the main streets. A small Ottoman college was incised into the Jewish cemetery to the east of the Byzantine gate, the beginning of what would become the nucleus of the Aristotle University of Thessaloniki that today occupies the center of the former graveyard. In 1908 the Young Turks proclaimed a republic in Plateia Eleutheria and for three days this square was the center of the empire where the Committee of Union and Progress, comprising the mélange of nationalities that made up the population of this metropolitan city, began its prophetic and fateful journey to Istanbul. Soon, as a result of the first of the Balkan Wars (1912–13), Salonika was cut off from its traditional hinterland and became the northern outpost of an expanding Greek kingdom.

With events escalating quickly into World War I the city became strategically important and during this period was occupied by six different armies. As a result, Salonika underwent important political, economic and social changes. The Greek prime minister Venizelos, established his provisional government there and opened the city to the Allied forces enabling them continually to probe the soft underbelly of the Central Powers. This planned front, delayed by the disastrous Dardanelles adventure, was implemented after the Gallipoli failure of 1915, and so for the next three years thousands of soldiers interacted with thousands of local Salonikans in a polyglot wartime cacophony. Army camps were built, which after the war became slum quarters. Swamps were drained, roads were built, and miles of trenches were dug. The war economy made fortunes for many locals and it was generally a good time for the population. In 1917, however, a freak firestorm destroyed the commercial center of the Ottoman city with its centuries-old Jewish quarter. The Jewish community never recovered from that disaster. In 1918 the armies of the Entente broke through the Bulgarian defenses and so hastened the end of the war. More sinister invasions, however, were on the far horizon.

Meanwhile Greece continued to maintain its irredentist stance, known as the 'Megali Idea,'[1] after World War I. With British encouragement the Greeks invaded Turkey itself, but Kemal Ataturk and Ismet Inönü halted their advance deep in the Anatolian plateau and the ensuing retreat quickly turned into a rout. The Turks burned Smyrna and avenged Greek excesses with a slaughter of their own. The subsequent Treaty of Sèvres between Greece and Turkey called for an exchange of populations, the first of the postwar political solutions to ethnic rivalry. Venizelos took the opportunity to direct the overflow of Anatolian Greeks to Salonika. His aim was to Hellenize the city whose prewar economy had been dominated by the Jews, who constituted the majority of its population. Salonika, ravaged by the great fire of 1917, was being rebuilt as a modern Greek metropolis by the Greek government. Its economy, already crippled by the exodus of its middle-class entrepreneurs (many of them Jews) and by the influx of refugees during the war, now had to cope with tens of thousands of destitute but commercially astute Anatolian Greeks.

Salonika had literally exploded into the twentieth century, but who would govern her and reap the profits of the entrepôt of the Balkans and which recently independent Balkan nationality would succeed in capturing this cosmopolitan prize emerging like a phoenix from the detritus of the Ottoman Balkans? And would its Jewish majority support Greek control, work for a return of Ottoman sovereignty and their long-standing autonomy, or opt for the Austrian and French plan for a free port, perhaps similar to the status later awarded to Danzig? A number of these questions were resolved by the Balkan Wars and by World War I. Serbia had its hands full with the new Yugoslavia that it now dominated. Bulgaria had been defeated and pushed back beyond the Rhodope Mountains. Austro-Hungary no longer existed. The last vestige of the Ottoman Empire after its dissolution was the welcome that the retired sultan received in Jewish Salonika. Now the question was: How would the Greek government and local authorities act towards Salonika's Jewish population?

But how could all this help the huddled masses of Baron Hirsch, whose lifestyle, poor to begin with, declined during the economic chaos of the 1920s? Could they reap a meal from the labor hired to rebuild the destroyed city center? Could they find work among the archaeological crews now excavating the ancient agora and forum that stretched from the shore past the historic Via Egnatia? Could they hold their own as laborers and small shopkeepers in the face of government efforts to aid the Anatolian Greeks to gain an economic foothold in the city? In 1924, Sunday was designated a rest day, which forced the Jews to open their shops on the Sabbath, while the emphasis on Greek language struck at the four centuries of Sephardi culture that had dominated the city. Store signs now had to be in Greek, or be taxed. The traditional school system was under constant pressure to increase the Greek content of the curriculum. Poverty and disease proceeded apace during the 1920s and 1930s. As the poor increased in population their health deteriorated from the endemic malaria and pandemic tuberculosis.

There arose a traditional means of escape from this misery. The rich of course suffered little. Many left with their wealth for France where Sephardi colonies appeared and flourished until the Nazis deported them to Auschwitz in 1942.[2] Those who remained profited from the surfeit of labor and great new enterprises appeared. For the poor, relief came in two forms. First came the patronage of the upper classes, who collected moneys both at home and abroad – particularly from the American Joint Distribution Committee – and used it for relief and philanthropy. New quarters appeared called prosaically '151' or Kambel, a colloquialization of Camp Bell which the British had occupied during the war prior to the breakthrough of the Bulgarian defenses by the Serbs and Greeks that began the road to German surrender. The poor Jews of Kambel would suffer an urban riot in 1932, which contributed to the migration of thousands of Jews to Palestine during the next few years.

Relief came in other forms of escapism. The poor pursued sports, collectively as in soccer and individually through boxing or wrestling. In boxing, the Salonikan Jews in partcular excelled both locally and regionally; winning the Balkan Middleweight Championship as well as local Greek honors. These youth still had hope, a residual theme of Jewish tradition continuously stressed by the variety of schooling available. This included traditional religious schools, whether attached to synagogues, or independent; a community-supported educational system; the schools established by foreign nationals to spread their influence, namely Italian, French, German, American, etc., each with their religious and national counterparts. Among the latter the Alliance Israélite Universelle schools, the Jewish counterpart of the French *mission civilatrice*, were specifically aimed at the modernization of Jewish youth. And, of course, there was the national Greek school system, which the government actively promoted as its primary tool to hellenize the city and foster a new identity for the recently conquered north, the last 'success' of the Megali Idea.

The working poor found solace in tavernas and coffee-houses where they could sit for hours playing backgammon and smoking cigarettes. Soon cannabis hemp or hashish became readily available as a popular export from Lebanon to compete with the local Balkan tobacco. Together with cheap retsina and endless political talk, the stage was set for the introduction of a new form of music, a local variant of the spreading Balkan jazz that was to permeate the ports from Romania to Cairo and throughout the Aegean. In the 1930s, Bazouki, as the Greeks called it, became popular in the coffee-houses while the wider phenomenon of Rembetika characterized the newly emerging underworld. Its themes were common to American jazz: drugs, poverty, lost loves, whores and houris, and jail where a man could suffer the pangs of conscience or lament the brutalities of the local police.

Into this fermenting reservoir of poor Jews with a rich cultural heritage and of poor Christians yearning for economic security and a new identity in the freedom of a Christian Greek state the two new ideologies of Fascism and Communism infiltrated, to compete with the Athens-directed Greek nationalism. The Greek monarchy, in the meantime, was challenged by a military out of control and a republicanism that would be resolved only some three decades after World War II amid continuing civil strife. Poverty drew adherents to both ideologies since the one promised salvation through power, as witnessed by the successes of Mussolini and later Hitler, while the other promised a messianic resolution to the question of poverty through a

classless and moneyless society. The new ingredients only embittered
a pot already seething with poverty exacerbated by ethnic competi-
tions which neither nationalism nor religion could resolve. The anti-
Semitism fomented by the Nazi Party found patches of support among
the Asiatic and Black Sea immigrants to Salonika who had brought
their own ancient antagonisms to the Jews with them alongside the
handful of prewar Greek anti-Semites (EEE) in the city.

The congeries of opposites that characterized Salonika in the inter-
war years were a contributing, albeit not a determining, factor in the
subsequent destruction of the Jewish community during the war. The
question is far more complex than the complexity of urban politics or
the theme of indifference that has characterized recent Holocaust writ-
ing.[3] Salonika, during the 40 years between 1912 and 1952, went
through the following catastrophic changes that completely changed
the composition and structure of the city from an Ottoman market center to a modern urban complex.

1. In 1912, a homogeneous Greek monarchy replaced the multi-
   ethnic Ottoman caliphate.
2. The fire of 1917 destroyed the central Jewish quarter.
3. Huge numbers of sophisticated immigrant Greeks resettled in 1923
   clashed with the entire local population.
4. The world stock market crash of 1929 crippled an already disastrous economic situation.
5. The civil strife between monarchists and republicans and between
   the religious and the revolutionary socialists militated against any
   peaceful solution – indeed they were only temporarily resolved by
   the dictatorship of Ioannis Metaxas and the Italian invasion.
6. The conquest by the Nazis and their brutal occupation.
7. The even more brutal occupation of Thrace by the Bulgarians that
   sent tens of thousands of refugees to Salonika.
8. The deportation and murder of nearly the entire Jewish population
   (*c.* 46,000) of the city.
9. The cruel civil war that pitted Greek against Greek (whatever their
   ethnic origin).
10. The persecution of the Left by the victorious Right that lasted until
    the 1970s. An interesting and important corollary to these seminal
    events is the emergence of the Greek woman out of the traditional
    patriarchalism of Greek society that even the persecutions of the
    1930s, 1940s, 1950s and 1960s could not abate.

To say, then, that the deportation of the Jews of Salonika was partly a result of the indifference of the population is to ignore the survival skills of the poor that ranged the gamut from passivity to revolutionary activism. This poor, each of whose constituents had witnessed or experienced death face to face through hunger, rape and sword, let alone having been the brunt of continuous persecution throughout the preceding generation, looked upon the removal of the Jews as perhaps just another element in the misery of the world. Among them were to be found those who supported the deportations as well as others – primarily the older Greek population that knew the local Jews – who regretted loss of friends and neighbors. The newcomers, however, outnumbered them, and even their attitudes were diverse. All of these factors then have to be entered into the question of the reaction of 'bystanders'. Moreover, the local politicians, the Church, and the regional leadership have to be analyzed in greater depth than has hitherto been done. Perhaps, then, an answer may be forthcoming to the question: Why did Salonika react differently from Athens during the occupation?[4] And finally, when this entire infrastructure has been clarified, we may return to the murderers themselves and ask why were the Jews deported when they were? It turns out that the local population and even the local German administration had little to do with the decision, whatever their attitude, or the timing. Those decisions were made in Berlin, Vienna and Auschwitz.[5]

Yitzhak Mosheh (Isaac Moissis) was born in Salonika on May 5, 1919 into a poor but socially active family residing in the Baron Hirsch quarter, a squalor that had been founded at the turn of the century to house East European refugees from pogroms in Kishinev and elsewhere. So chaotic were the social conditions of those Ashkenazi refugees that the sobriquet 'Ashkenazi' became the local Sephardi term for 'pimp'. His father was concerned with the continuing plight of the tobacco workers who were consistently exploited by agents and entrepreneurs to provide the quality hand-cut local tobaccos to the world market. Thousands of young men and women in Salonika and Kavalla earned a precarious living in this trade. Attempts had been made to organize them, especially through the Socialist Federation of Labor founded by Abraham Benaroya, but by the 1930s his efforts were being overshadowed by the new rhetoric of Communism.

Yitzhak Mosheh went to a Jewish school in Baron Hirsch and then attended the Collège des Frères, a French Catholic missionary school located in the city.[6] It was there as a teenager facing a life of poverty that he debated with himself whether to become a Catholic or a

Communist. At the time he chose neither. He then attended the Deutsche Schule to prepare for further study in Germany to become an engineer. The rise of Nazism and its anti-Semitism coupled with parental reservations convinced him that this was not a productive path. His critical decision-making moment came with the Metaxas coup and its anti-Communist stance; this convinced him to join an anti-fascist organization. In the beginning the group assisted the refugees from Asia Minor and those who had been exiled or jailed by the regime. He, along with Mosheh Benveniste and Ephraim Rosenberg, collected money for families, wrote slogans for the KKE, and sold copies of the KKE paper *Rizospastis* to tobacco workers and porters. Among his contacts were Avraham Sustiel, a syndicalist; Abraham Benaroya; Joseph Gattegno, who was a leader in the KKE; Saltiel; the Stroumza family; Michael Tiano; and Rosa Cohen, who became a Communist and later an *andartissa*.

On March 1, 1940 he was drafted into the Greek army, whereupon he was told that his name was on the army's watch list and that because of this he could not become an officer. He did basic training in Verroia and, after three months, was stationed in Kozani on the Albanian border. His unit remained on the front line for the next six months. It suffered during Mussolini's failed spring offensive, not through the latter's competence but through the venality of the commander of Company 50, Mandouvalos, whom Mosheh remembers as a 'fascist' and an anti-Semite. On March 9, Mandouvalos sent three units comprising a considerable Jewish presence, Companies 30, 31, and 16 (from Verroia), without any artillery support across the bridge at Trebesina that was covered by Italian fire. Not until April 1941, while still besieging Mount Trebesina, were they ordered to stand down and disarm by a German party announcing that Greece had surrendered. Moshe walked home, traversing over a thousand kilometers of occupied Greece. When he reached the bottleneck at the Kalambaka Bridge, near Meteora, he learned that the Germans were arresting many soldiers. Ever the loner, Mosheh backtracked to Larissa and took another route to Salonika only to find that on his returning there his home was occupied by Germans, forcing him to find refuge elsewhere. Eventually he met up with a number of prewar acquaintances and under their influence he drifted towards and then joined the Communist Party. Initially he was involved in distributing leaflets and organizing assistance for the famine victims[7] of the 1941–2 *Hungerwinter* during which over 100,000 victims are estimated to have died. The Germans responded to all incidents with collective punishment, and after the destruction of the Aksiopolis Bridge they shot 100 hostages from the Pavlos Melas Prison. Among these was Albert Carasso, the father of Daisy, who was later to marry Yitzhak Mosheh. Mosheh's last action in Salonika was to assist with the liquidation of an SS man who terrorized the Jewish Quarter and the neighboring Greeks.

After the forced registration of male Jews (aged 16—45) beginning on July 11, 1942 Mosheh was in a group of 100 Jews sent as slave laborers to the Vale of Tempi.[8] While there, the group was berated by a leader of the local resistance for not escaping to the hills to fight with the *andartes*; consequently Mosheh decided to escape. 'The Jews had no faith in such solutions. They had no direction. I had to act alone, and I always acted alone,' he recalled. He joined the *andartes* in Naousa where he was based with five or six men in a monastery occupied by one nun. At the beginning, lightly armed, they foraged for food in the fields. His rifle, salvaged from the war by a peasant, was stopped up by a rusted bullet, but only he knew that. The only other Jew that he met in his area was a Hebrew- and English-speaker named Abraham who, Mosheh suspected, might have been a Yemenite from Palestine who had been with the BEF.[9] The resistance around Naousa was mainly inactive save for sporadic actions until the end of March 1943.

Then on March 30, they received the order to enter the village of Papia near Naousa, liberate the silos and divide the wheat among the villagers. The following day, they learned that the gendarmes of Naousa were being transferred to Salonika, so with 85 armed men they attacked the Germans stationed there, capturing 4 (whom they soon released for fear of savage German reprisals) and seized all the weapons they could, enabling them to recruit more locals, among whom were a number of Greek army officers. The next day the Germans mounted a major attack on the *andartes*. They were driven off, but a Pole serving with the Germans was captured and he became an *andarte* until the liberation. This was the period, as Mosheh recalled, that many Jews joined the resistance (up till then he had been the only Jew in his area), the majority from Salonika who had taken refuge in Pieria and Paikos. By the beginning of April nearly a hundred had joined and by the end of April-beginning of May the number was close to 500, the majority of which were youths. They were for the most part unarmed as the *andartes* had only one submachine gun and one Thompson submachine gun that the Pole, whom they called Joseph, had contributed.

The Germans mounted a major attack on April 20 (Hitler's birthday) near the village of Outsena and one later in Kserolivada. The *andartes* suffered many casualties in both attacks, including the death of Salvator Ovadia. Kapetan Petros, Kitsos recalled, ordered him to retreat, but Kitsos replied, 'I want to see the Germans aiming at me!'[10]

At the beginning of May the Germans announced that they would grant an amnesty to anyone who laid down his arms. The group decided to leave Mount Naousa and crossed to Mount Grevena. Reaching the road to Kozani, they skirmished with a German patrol, and despite 80 percent of the men being unarmed they succeeded in killing 20 Germans, the remainder fleeing. The group then crossed into a liberated area where BLOs were already active.[11] At the village of Vlatsi, the BLOs supplied them with weapons (sub machine guns) and other supplies. At Dasmaskinya, where there was an airport, they were divided into units and ordered back to Vermion. Later a group that had become separated during the escape and had been captured by the Germans – but being unarmed they were given amnesty and subsequently released – rejoined the main body and all were armed. The men then began to engage in sabotage.

Hence, we cannot account for an organized and effective resistance movement for the region including Mounts Naousa, Grevena, Vermion before late May 1943. But according to Mosheh's affidavit, we should find our largest concentration of Jewish *andartes* in this region of Greek Macedonia. We recall from the Introduction that Joseph Matsas had estimated some 650 Jewish fighters in the mountains, and we had increased that to about a thousand based on reports and data of which he was not aware. Most sources aver that about 450 Salonikans served with ELAS and a number of *andartes* recall serving with many Jews in their units. Indeed, Mosheh emphasizes that Jews participated in every action with him and a number were killed having fought to the last bullet.[12] The question is how many other Jews served, beyond those whom we shall meet in later chapters, from other areas of Greece. The material collected by Michael Matsas suggests a concentration of Jews in the 50th, 16th, 24th, and 54th regiments and the II Division (11/34 and Y/34 battalions) of ELAS which fought in Attika and Boeotia.[13] But let us follow Mosheh's testimony further and see where it leads us concerning the question of Jewish numbers in the *andartiko*. The figure for Jewish fighters quoted above does not include the many who participated in the widespread social revolution in the mountains. Mosheh avers an extensive organization in both the cities and the villages, and on every front able to supply money, requisition food and supplies, enlist recruits, care for *andarte* families, assist Jews who were homeless refugees, let alone undertake education and political reeducation and other activities (See Daisy Carasso's report ch. 3). After the war nearly 10,000 Jews came out of the mountains to a Greece ready to engage in the next stage of civil war.[14]

The fighting, however, concentrated on sabotage, control of roads, destruction of bridges, and protection of the harvest from the Germans. Mosheh – now known by his *nom de guerre* 'Kitsos' – became a *politikos* and led first a platoon then a company. There were constant attacks on collaborators whom the Germans armed against the 'communists', a blanket term used by the Germans to smear the multiple leftist ideologies represented by EAM, all of whom rejected the occupation of their *patrida* (native land).

The resistance became much better armed after the surrender of the Italians in September 1943. One whole division, the Pinerolo, surrendered and joined the partisans; those who were unwilling to fight were dispersed among the villages. In mid October they were disarmed by ELAS.[15] The new weapons allowed for increased recruiting. Kitsos participated in a battle against the Italians and some Germans who were also in the vicinity, at Kastoria. They destroyed the bridge at the village of Tsouka and harassed the enemy forces. At Kastoria, the headquarters for the Slavo-Macedonians, Kitsos captured the deputy to the leader of the collaborators Anton Kaltchev, and handed him over for interrogation, where he was proven to be a spy.[16] There was also an attempt to kill the German commander in Ardea. The Yugoslav partisans assisted in that operation by keeping a full company at the rear to ensure a safe retreat; in general the Yugoslav partisans offered moral support for ELAS in the mountains they both shared.

A major action against the Germans took place at Kostohori at the end of September 1943 when two truckloads of SS were ambushed and killed. As it became clearer to what extent the German position had been undermined by the defeat at Stalingrad, more pressure was exerted to close and control the roads; one of ELAS's goals was to close the Kastania Road near Kozani. The Germans, for their part, increased their attacks to keep the roads open but suffered heavy casualties in the process. Daisy Carasso's brother, Lieutenant Marco Carasso, was particularly active in these battles and was killed at Muharram Han (see below) where some 250 Germans also fell. In the mountains of Jzena near Yugoslavia, the Germans suffered many dead, including a general.

At the village of Kerasia, Kitsos and a handful of men inflicted heavy casualties on a German force that attacked them. He was recognized as a national hero for that action.

From there he returned to attack the German headquarters located at Verroia. He and his 17 men inflicted heavy casualties and got away unscathed; but the Germans shot 50 Greeks in reprisal. Around April 20, 1944 the Germans assembled some 110,000 heavily armed men to reopen the mountain roads. Kitsos, located at the time in the village of Megarama near Edessa, was ordered to stand and fight. They fought, dispersed, and regrouped. He was then ordered, along with five or six others, to deal with collaborators, and he spent the next few months arresting them and bringing them to ELAS headquarters. Recalling his sabotage missions, Kitsos explained that when an operation was imminent a planner would come from headquarters and discuss it with him. Once the plan was agreed, Kitsos would gather together a force of five or six men and send for support from the army. By this time the resistance army was fully organized and numbered, according to Kitsos, 60,000–80,000 regulars with a reserve of around 200,000 men. His base was in the Vale of Angelohori, where he hid in the fields for two months and participated in numerous battles for control of the harvest. In July 1944 he was ordered back to Mount Grevena where he engaged in a battle in the surrounding area near the villages of Batala and Perivolo in which his commander 'Papaflessa' was killed.[17] Without thinking about the question of authority or of the consequences Kitsos gave the order to attack the Germans, who subsequently suffered heavy casualties. Earlier British help was by now being supplemented, as he recalled, with help from both Canadian and Russian liaison officers.

In addition to regular fighting with the Germans, ELAS had to deal with ethnic revolts against the Greeks stirred up by the Axis. Kitsos also had to deal with a *Kapetan* Zissis and his 'international' brigade which he described as consisting of Italians, Tatars, and Senegalese. This type of jockeying for power would keep the area in turmoil for decades and complicate scholarship for generations. A bloody battle at Pelargos involved Turkish-speaking Greeks (from Pontus and Caucasia). The village was split between the Greek-speaking Greeks who supported ELAS and the Turkish-speaking Greeks who supported the Germans.[18] Kitsos considers them to be the best fighters he encountered. Among the heavy losses suffered by both sides was their commander General Babagiorgi, who was wounded and died in the arms of Kitsos who then buried him.[19]

In October 1944 the Germans were well advanced in their retreat from Greece. While they had already discussed an agreement with the British to leave Athens and the Peloponnesus without fighting, no such understanding was forthcoming for the north.[20] Their plan was to open the road to Salonika and from there to continue north through Bulgaria. Thus they would have to pass through Kitsos's territory, over the network of roads that ELAS controlled via Verroia and Naousa. An ambush at the village of Stavro near Verroia led to a major battle in perhaps the last area of Greece to remain under German control. It was there that Kitsos lost Charles Bourlas, the younger brother of Yolanda. His body was never recovered. Kitsos sadly recalled this loss, for he was proud of his reputation as a leader who cared for the safety and survival of his men. Indeed he never lacked for volunteers. He once asked the men why they were quick to volunteer for his missions and their reply was, 'Because we know you will bring us back alive.'[21]

NOTES

1. Based on the nineteenth-century Hellenic irredentism of the Athens Kingdom.
2. Serge Klarsfeld, *Le memorial de la deportation des Juifs de France* (Paris, 1978), convoi nos. 44 and 45 (November 1942). See my 'The Great Powers and the Jews: British and French Consuls on Interwar Greek Jewry', *Proceedings of the World Congress of Jewish Studies*, Division B, Volume II (Jerusalem, 1990), pp. 379–86.
3. George Mavrogordatos, *Stillborn Republic: Social Conditions and Party Strategies in Greece, 1922–1936* (Berkeley, 1983); Raul Hilberg, *Perpetrators, Victims and Bystanders* (New York, 1992); Andrew Apostolou, '"The Exception of Salonika": Bystanders and Collaborators in Northern Greece,' *Holocaust and Genocide Studies* 14 (fall, 2000), pp. 165–96.
4. The circumstances of the occupation in both cities were entirely different: Italians in Athens and Germans in Salonika; the sophistication and organization of the Left leadership in Athens; the differing attitudes of the Germans before and after Stalingrad; the role of the Allies in the south as opposed to the north; and the status of the resistance after the deportations, as well as a number of additional factors.
5. See my 'The timing of the deportations of the Jews,' in *Macedonia and Thrace, 1941–1944. Occupation-Resistance-Liberation. International Conference (9–11 December 1994)* (Thessaloniki, 1998), pp. 221–9.
6. His story is based on the transcript of a five-hour tape of his interview at Yad Vashem in April 1988 (YVS 03/4542) and several interviews with the author in March and December 1997. Mosheh was careful to emphasize that he related only those actions to which he could attest and that his remarks were restricted to his own participation. This strengthens the historical usefulness of his interviews.
7. Mark Mazower, *Inside Hitler's Greece. The Experience of Occupation, 1941–1944* (New Haven and London, 1993); Ch. 3 focuses primarily on Athens. The situation was worse in Salonika, especially among the urbanized Jewish community, which had little connection with the villages. See Steven Bowman (ed.) *The Holocaust in Salonika. Eyewitness Accounts* (New York, 2002) for details.
8. Other Jews were sent to the chrome mines in Chalkidiki or to repair the railroad in Larissa and Thebes. There were other labor camps as well where Jews and Greeks were interned;

however, it was Nazi occupation policy to strip the Jewish community of all able-bodied men and especially intellectuals. The latter rarely survived the forced labor battalions. For the reaction of the Jewish Community to the forced labor policy, see the detailed report of Yomtov Yacoel in *The Holocaust in Salonika. Eyewitness Accounts*. Mosheh recalls that the brother of Albert Carasso died of malaria there.

9. Nearly 2,500 Palestinians (some 2,000 Jews and 400 Arabs) were with the BEF in Greece. A number of Yemenite Jews are recorded and a few were with the resistance (see YVS 03/2703 and summary in John O. Iatrides (ed.), *Greece in the 1940s. A Bibliographic Companion* (Hanover, NH and London, 1981), p. 87).

10. There are a number of letters from Yitshak Mosheh ('Kitsos') in the archive of Joseph Matsas testifying to the friendship that the two had developed after Kitsos's visit to Greece in the 1980s. These letters supplement the interviews noted above. My thanks to Allegra Matsas for reading these with me.

11. The British Harling Mission came in October 1942 to blow up the Gorgopotamos Bridge (November 25) and remained to organize the resistance. See E.C.W. Myers, *Greek Entanglement* (rev. edn Gloucester, 1985).

12. In one of his letters to Joseph Matsas, Kitsos lists the following battles in which he took part: Naousa, where a small unit of *andartes* took 90 guns from the enemy; Ipapandis; Outsena; Kserolivado; Bithos near Kastoria; Amoudaris; Kastoria (against Italians and 'bourgaroanoi'); Kazovaka, where he blew up bridges; Megarema; Theodorakio at Ardea; Kerasia, where with seven *andartes* he chased away a German platoon; Verroia; Andera, where they cleared the Germans from Paiko; Arkoudoxore or Angeloxore; Kilkis (Nov. 4 1944); Pelargos, Audela; and Perivolo. See n. 19.

13. Jewish commanders led a number of units in this theater: Sam Askenazi was company commander of 10/54 Regiment; Benjamin Negrin headed a platoon in 1/38 Regiment; 'Skoufos' a platoon in 11/34 Battalion; and Marco Carasso a platoon in the 16th Regiment.

14. See CZA 5/64571, which contains a list of cities in 1946 totaling 8,489 Jews, 867 of whom were returnees from Poland. Already several boatloads of Jews had left for Palestine.

15. For their fate, see Richard Lamb, *War in Italy 1943–1945. A Brutal Story* (New York, 1996), pp. 152 f. See Iatrides, *Greece in the 1940s*.

16. Cf. John S. Koliopoulos, *Plundered Loyalties. World War II and Civil War in Greek West Macedonia* (New York, 1999), *passim*. There were two postwar trials in Thessalonika of Anton Kaltchev, who was born a Slavo-Macedonian in the village of Spilaia, grew up in Bulgaria, and served as a lieutenant in the Bulgarian forces that liaised with the Germans in Thessaloniki and the Italians in Kastoria (pp. 64 f.); for his fate see p. 66 n. He was indeed more than a spy; he was an important figure in the ethnic–political rivalry over the area of Macedonia. Koliopoulos does not mention the capture of Kaltchev's deputy by ELAS.

17. Both Papaflessa and Kitsos were heroes of the War of Independence of 1821, although Mosheh took his *nom de guerre* from the captain under whom he served in Albania.

18. On the impossible situation that the mixed villages faced in the interstice between EAM–ELAS and the Axis, see Koliopoulos, *Plundered Loyalties*, pp. 72–73.

19. Another Jewish *andarte*, Morris Hayyim, told Kitsos that the doctor erred in binding Babagiorgi's wound, thus allowing an infection to develop. Hayyim stepped on a mine during the civil war and was killed.

20. The Swedish Red Cross representative Hans Ehrenstrale informed me of his role as intermediary in Patras and Edgar Thomashausen informed me of his role as official intermediary in Athens in 1941 and 1944. The scholarly controversy over such agreements hinges on the lack of documentary evidence. Nonetheless the withdrawals from the urban centers were carried out with minimal harassment. See Lars Bærentzen, 'Liberation of the Peloponnese', in John O. Iatrides (ed.), *Greece in the 1940s*. (Hanover and London, 1981), p. 139. For Athens, see Stefanos Serafis, *ELAS: Greek Resistance Army* (London, 1980), p. 412.

21. Sarafis, *ELAS*, ends his litany of actions on October 31, 1944. None of the above actions are listed by Sarafis who admits however, that his extensive list is not complete. Kitsos continued to fight beyond that date. Pursing the Germans north, ELAS caught up with them on November 4, 1944 at Kilkis, some 40 kilometers north of Salonika. ELAS slaughtered the German forces and the collaborators who were escaping with them. A virtual

massacre, Kitsos recalls, regrettable, but necessary. Kitsos recalled a short list of some of the Jewish *andartes* that fought with him: Yitzhak Emanuel; Yitzhak Rousso; Ya'akov Levi ('Perikles'); 'Eriko Pipano'; Isak Ovadia from Czechoslovakia; Danny Ovadia who fell in battle at Sporgiti?; Shabtai Hasson, Avram Varon; Avram Hason; David Cohen; Saltiel; Morris Belo ('Maliaropolos'); Morris (Moshe) Pinhas; Mois Bourla; Charles Bourlas; Marcus Karasso, the three Cohen brothers; Hayyim ('Chico'), Morris, and Eli; Moshe Miyuni; Yona Miyuni; Roel Nissahon, Zaharias Cohen; Dariko who played the accordion; Attias from Kavalla; Isak Lazar; Salvator Lazar who was killed by a mine after the war; Raul Saias; Morris; Rula or Rahel Levi who was the wife of 'Perikles'; Kounio who was the brother of Sarah Kounio and was a pharmacist; and Morris Hayyim who was a pre-med student (the latter was also recalled by Fanny Florentin, see Afterword and in note 19).

3

Kapetanissa Sarika and the Euboea Portage

Many Greek-Jewish memoirs recall the solidarity of Jewish families and the unwillingness of young Jews to abandon their parents who, they thought, were going to a new and strange home in the Kingdom of Krakovia. It was also difficult for city boys and girls to adjust to the rough life in the mountains.

Daisy Carasso (born 1926) was educated in a Greek public school but because of the war completed only a few years of high school. Of all her male relatives, only her father and younger brother were not drafted during the war. In April 1941 the Germans entered Salonika and began to confiscate Jewish businesses, among them the Molho bookstore, which was the largest in Macedonia, and her father lost his job as its manager. During the mass arrests of the summer, he was taken hostage and after 18 months in various jails he was shot on December 30, 1942 in reprisal for the destruction of a bridge by the resistance. His son Marko (Mordecai in Hebrew) was given his watch by students who worked in the prison. They told him his father's last words were that he protect the family and that he join the resistance to fight against the Germans. Many of Daisy's father's and brother's friends joined the *andartiko*, while Marko went into hiding with Christian friends during the continued roundups for forced labor. He eventually began recruiting for the resistance and Daisy acted as his liaison with the young men he persuaded to join. When she went to arrange for the latter to escape to the mountains, however, she recalls being chased away by the family matriarchs.[1] A number of her friends who were active in Zionist youth movements also joined the resistance.

In early April 1943 Daisy Carasso[2] left for the mountains with her mother and her young sister, an arrangement made by a Jew who was friendly with a black marketeer, who was also the local recruiter for the Communist Party and the *andartiko* from the village of Dafni near Negrita.[3] After a number of adventures, including passing off her mother as a long-term resident of France to account for her peculiar Greek accent, they reached the village of Todorakia where the local teacher played host to them through Easter. When an informer appeared, the local policeman warned them to escape; they left for Kilkis where the doorman for their building in Salonika lived. Without documents they had to return to the villages. Eventually they reached Negrita where she joined the resistance. Such experiences illustrate the reasons why more Jews, especially among the poor, did not escape to the mountains.

Negrita, with its population of about 9,000, was the center for ELAS Regiment 19.[4] Daisy joined EPON, where she helped to prepare food and clothes, and assisted the families of *andartes* in the 22 villages surrounding Serres and Negrita. She also helped recruit young men, did guard duty, carried ammunition, and distributed leaflets and propaganda in Negrita.[5] There were demonstrations on national holidays and once, when the Germans and Bulgarians tried to break up one such demonstration by shooting at it, she led the young girls in a dance around the monument to the Unknown Soldier, singing the death song of the Suliote women from the 1821 War of Independence.

There were many young women who served in various ways with the resistance, both in the cities and in the mountains, from gatherers of information to fighters. Women were particularly adept at masquerading as prostitutes, although the guild of Greek prostitutes in Athens had loyally refused to offer their services to the conquerors in the aftermath of the German victory. When hunger forced them to reevaluate their stance, they began to collect information, which was passed along to independent and central groups who forwarded the information to Cairo. A number of young girls, including several Jews, volunteered as escorts to Wehrmacht officers in order to absorb information via the well-known tactic of 'pillow talk'. But it was mainly Greek-Christian women who organized these nets, many of whom have become legendary in resistance annals.

Since there was a greater danger for young Jewish women if caught, as they were shot or sent to Poland, most went to the mountains. Yad Vashem, during its debriefings of immigrants since the 1950s, has collected a good number of Greek memoirs over the past half-century. These depositions contain considerable detail on the resistance and deserve further study; a few of them are germane to our story.

Jewish girls served in a number of ways that belied their rather genteel urban upbringing and high level of education. Also, they came from a patriarchal society that protected its women from too much contact with the harsh realities of Balkan public life. Nevertheless the girls received excellent education whether in Spanish, French, Italian, German, or Greek culture. Many of them were polyglot with a keen interest in the outside world into which they increasingly entered during the inter-war period.

Matilda Bourla, for example, became interested in nursing after seeing a film about Florence Nightingale. She subsequently left Salonika to visit her uncle in Athens who helped her enter training at the city's Elpis Hospital. Matilda worked there until she was threatened with arrest by the Gestapo after the Germans took over the Italian zone in September 1943. She was rescued by none other than the king's personal physician who helped her to escape to the mountains above Thebes, where she assisted at a resistance hospital. When German patrols threatened to overrun the site, the nurses moved their patients higher up the mountain, each one carrying a wounded man on her back for several hours. To this day she still suffers from back pains and rheumatism, She was awarded medals by both France and Greece for her actions. Many Jewish nurses served with the Greek Red Cross during the war against Italy in 1940–1. A number of them later served with the resistance, whether EAM in the cities or its military wing ELAS in the mountains.

In the cities of the Italian zone, where Jews, especially women, were not persecuted, they acted as runners, contacts, and smugglers of weapons and propaganda. Others were able to communicate with the occupiers and so assist in the rescue of threatened resistance activists. Some joined the resistance; women in particular acted as escorts for Axis officers and so contributed to the flow of information that flooded British intelligence centers.

Many women were part of the fighting units of ELAS that preached liberating the female sex from the bonds of patriarchalism. This revolutionary message was reluctantly supported by male villagers, along with the new society that EAM–ELAS had introduced into the mountains it controlled, and they would quickly reject it after the war. The Greek Right and the British condemned the Left resistance as communist and so made it easier for the men of the villages to regain control over their women. Tens of thousands, however, refused to give up their belief in the liberation of women and many spent a decade or two after the war in prison by refusing to recant their participation in the resistance and its revolution.

World War II opened a new chapter in warfare with the appearance of women fighters, particularly in the Communist-dominated partisan movements. While there were some hard-core Communists among them, most of the women were socialist-leaning educated girls who recruited village girls or were themselves refugees from Axis persecution. Morality was more than strict. The army protected their virtue by threatening violators with death. However, it did allow partisans to marry each other and provided a village priest for that purpose.

Several Jewish women are particularly interesting, especially since Jews do not appear in the general literature about the resistance or, in particular, in recent studies about the women of the *andartiko*. Dora Bourla fought in the mountains of Macedonia and was known as 'Tarzan' to her fellow fighters. Another, Dora (Raban) was part of a female fighting unit of 30 women. At the end of the war in Greece she was rescued from this group by a Jewish *andartis* who told her that the Communist leadership had decided to ship this unit to Korea as a sign of solidarity. Dora was fortunate; all of them, as she recalled, were killed in Korea.

Other young Jewish girls through force of personality rose to positions of importance within ELAS. C.K. (Carmen Kakis) from Drama, for example, whose redheaded beauty was matched only by the sweetness of her singing voice, was a *kapetanissa*, with responsibility for recruiting women for the resistance.[6] She was also sent several times by the resistance to the Island of Skopelos for periods of rest.[7] There she stayed with Lily Mitrani, a teacher from Salonika who had asked the Greek government for a transfer to a safer locale where she could teach openly as a Jew, which she was able to do on Skopelos throughout the war. She was also in the underground, and for that reason was able to provide the resistance with such periodic hospitality.[8]

After the German evacuation from Greece, western journalists accompanied the British and Greek forces that replaced them. We shall later encounter reports from British and Palestinian reporters. Here we shall cite the story of a *kapetanissa* as reported by the intrepid American Greek correspondent, Constantine Poulos, who entered Greece in mid-August 1944 and was already in Athens the day before the British forces arrived.[9]

> Athens, Oct. 23.(ONA – By Wireless) – Sarika Y——, 18-year old Jewish Greek girl from the city of Chalkis, is the captain of a company of uniformed women Andartes (Greek guerrillas) on the island of Euboea.
>
> Wearing a pair of British soldier boots and a cap, jacket and culotte uniform made from an American blanket, she leads her company daily in doing whatever job the Andarte regiment to which it is attached orders.

She is a short, stocky girl with dark hair and blue eyes. She runs like a man and can shoot a walnut from a tree at 200 yards. Whether she is calling out marching orders with a steady 'Hep, Hep, Hep' or pounding out a beat with her arm as her Company goes singing down a mountain path, she does it vibrantly and proudly.

Only after the Greek surrender to the Italians was it necessary for her to flee to the mountains. From there, as a peasant, she periodically went back to German-held Chalcis to gather information for her Andarte regiment. When this became too dangerous, she began teaching in mountain schools. Following this, she went to work in the Resistance Movement's central office. And later when a women's Andarte Company was organized, she was selected as its Captain.

Of a large family of sisters and brothers-in-law and uncles, only she and her mother are left. 'This is my country,' Sarika told me, 'I was born and raised here. The Greeks are my people, their fight is my fight. This is where I belong.'

Sarika is one of the incredible number of Greek women who took part in the fierce Resistance Movement. Sometimes it seems as if more women than men were in the mountains.[10]

I have watched organizers, cooks, laundresses, social workers and nurses tirelessly carrying out their tasks under the most difficult of conditions. They worked 10 to 12 hours a day organizing women's relief committees, schools, nurseries, clinics and hospitals, in those parts of Greece in Andarte hands.

I watched a demonstration of 4,000 women and 17 priests, who had gathered from a 25-mile radius, as they fearlessly approached a Nazi-held village to demand the release of dozens of hostages. They failed, but when I left, they were discussing their tactical errors and were planning a large mass demonstration by calling on more women from other villages.

In Roumeli, Crete, many people told me the story of Ariadne Dalari, a woman dentist from the Greek city of Lamia, who was tortured for fifteen days by the Nazis in an attempt to make her talk about the Resistance Movement. Unable to break her, they stood her against the wall and shot her while a crowd of women stood by, defiantly singing Andarte songs.

They also tell the story of another woman from Roumeli, Angelica Montesantou, who was condemned to death for underground activities. On the public scaffold, she placed the noose around her neck herself, tightened it, and shouted, 'I die happy because I die for my country.'

I watched a women's relief organization go from village to village collecting food and old clothes for those families whose houses had been burned by the Germans. After the Nazis had passed through, I saw women dig up sacks of wheat from their hiding places under the dirt floors of their homes. In other places, I have seen women carrying food and ammunition to isolated Andarte guard posts and garrisons.

Poulos was an active and aggressive correspondent who had a good eye and could write well. Without a doubt he took home many other good stories with him that he did not find the time to analyze or write down. He was the first, however, to record for the Allies, still at war, the story of the heroic women who served Greece during the occupation. Other stories and analyses were provided 50 years on by Altamarino, Hart, and Fourtouni among others.[11] The stories of Jewish women, however, have remained in oral memory or were buried in postwar depositions or hard-to-find Hebrew publications.

Sarika's image was well known to Allied journalists, although Poulos is the only one to have interviewed her and recorded her Jewish identity. As a result of the postwar persecution of former *andartes*, Sarika immigrated to Palestine in 1946 where she returned to a more sedentary life. This former *kapetanissa* at ELAS headquarters in Euboea married Marcello Fortis and raised a family. She was later interviewed for the Israeli record, and it appears from the following summary that Poulos only got a superficial look at this rather remarkable teenager.

Sarika was an excellent student and prominent as a youth leader in her high school in Halkis, the capital city of Evvoia. Born Sara Yehoshua she was the niece of Lieutenant Colonel Mordecai Frizis who died at Premeti leading the charge against the Italian invaders. Only 15 she escaped with her mother to the hills on a donkey and took refuge in the village of Sateni where she taught the women to read and write and to waken their female consciousness. Such activities were a central part of the resistance movement's participation in the social revolution that permeated the Greek hinterland during the war, and were performed by the young women of EPON. When she was informed that the Germans were sweeping through the area, her contact took her to the mountains where she began to serve more actively. Sporting two bandoleers, she moved through the villages explaining the resistance to the women and eventually succeeded in organizing a unit of young women to serve first as camp auxiliaries working in the mess, laundry, etc. Later they were taught to handle weapons and to make 'Molotov cocktails' (gasoline-filled bottles that exploded into flames on contact). British observers would later note in amazement the anomaly of the tiny young woman who paraded two-meter tall male fighters for their benefit.

At the beginning of 1944 they were ready for action. *Kapetanissa* Sarika and her 12 handpicked girls became a special diversion squad for the resistance. When an action was planned against the Germans, Sarika and her unit, armed with 'Molotov cocktails', were sent to a distant village where they simulated an attacking force. The Germans responded; the girls melted away since they were above suspicion; and the main resistance force carried out its action elsewhere. Once she was sent by her commanding officer to the village of Kabia where the local priest was a German informer. Dressed in peasant garb Sarika shyly told him she had a confession to make but was too embarrassed to reveal it in such a holy place. When he left the church, the *andartes* arrested him. The story spread quickly throughout the area and the reputation of the unit and its Jewish leader was accordingly enhanced.

When the Germans learned that 'the teacher' was operating out of the village of Sateni, they sent an informer to flush her out. It turned out however that he caught Sarika's cousin, Medi Moskowitz, who was also a teacher. His mistake was that he asked for 'the teacher.' The Germans arrested her and destroyed the house where she was hiding. The informer was given the privilege of murdering Medi, but she was first brutally abused and tortured. Sarika, hearing of the tragedy, asked her commander for permission to avenge the deed. The *andartes* verified the identity of the informer and Sarika went to the village. On the way she encountered the informer and asked him about her cousin. He replied, 'Finally we are rid of the Jewish teacher.' She took out her revolver and shot him. This act too added to her legend locally.

In another incident word came that the Germans were planning a *razzia* in the environs of Halkis. She was sent to warn them, so she climbed onto a roof and with a megaphone called on the villages to flee to the *andartes*. Her teenage voice found a response and the young males fled to the resistance. After the Germans retreated from Greece, she returned to Chalkis where she continued to work with young people. Since the former *andartes* were out of favor with the new leaders of Greece, Sara was soon arrested; however, her reputation saved her.

The police investigator warned her to hurry to the local rabbi and ask him to send her to Athens whence she could leave Greece. Since 1946 she has lived in the environs of Tel Aviv where she raised her family.

Evvoia, during the war, was the assembly point for Jewish refugees from Athens (mainly survivors from Salonika who either fled before the deportations or escaped with foreign papers under the aegis of the Italian authorities there) who embarked on caiques for the Turkish port of Çesme. This 'underground' ferry service, one of several to ply the Aegean escape route, had been organized by two brothers, one in Athens and the other in Izmir, in conjunction with the Palestinian Jewish defense forces, the Hagganah, and under the protection of ELAS. Ultimately it would be responsible for the rescue of over 1,000 Jews and several important non-Jewish Greeks, including George Papandreou a future prime minister.

Evvoia is an elongated island that hugs the coast of Central Greece. It is divided from the mainland by the volcanic action that supplies the hot springs of Thermopylai and generates the shift of current that so perplexed Aristotle. The northern end faces Volos and the southern end with its string of islands that lead to the archipelago beckons Attika with its mountains and beaches. It was to the mountains that the Jews of Halkis, the capital of the island, fled for safety and where most of them survived. Jewish mothers from Volos crossed to the northern end of the island and parceled out their children among the mountain villagers for the duration of the war. And it was via Oropos that Jews from Athens, including numerous refugees from Salonika, crossed to Evvoia for the long trek to safety in Asia Minor and the Levant. In addition to the sanctuary that Evvoia provided, there was its importance as a transit between Attika and Turkey. Traffic ran in both directions with recruits and refugees moving east across the Aegean and Greek and British officers moving west via various carriers into occupied Greece.

The complicated story of resistance and collaboration, rescue and betrayal, heroism and cowardice that constituted the wartime experience of Evvoia will not be recounted here. Rather, the organization of the rescue of (primarily) Jews emerges from the records in the Hagganah Archives in Tel Aviv. It may be best to begin by describing the raw material that filtered in on a regular basis to the Jewish Agency desks in Jerusalem. This data consisted of information obtained from the debriefing of refugees who had successfully crossed the Aegean and made it to Palestine. They were debriefed along the way by a variety of agencies.[12] The material was then forwarded to Jerusalem where

general statements were constructed from the data for public con-
sumption and for the British and Jewish agencies in Cairo. More secret
data – names of potential aid-givers or potential dangermongers – were
extracted for briefing agents going to mainland Greece and in preparation for postwar use. It is to be emphasized that the Greek gentile iden-
tifications are to be read with caution: some of the names are clearly
aliases; others have lost their identification in the vicissitudes of copy-
ing; while others may be the result of hearsay.

The Evvoia–Çesme route, which wove through the patchwork of
Aegean islands, was already in operation by smugglers before the war.
During the negotiations between the British and the Nazis, mediated
through the ICRC, over the question of supplying the Greeks with
enough food in light of the impending famine, it was agreed that
Turkish wheat would be sent to Greece on Swedish ships flying the
ICRC flag. We know now that the British took advantage of this agreement (in addition to other avenues) to smuggle agents into Greece; the
Germans probably knew or at least suspected as much. Nonetheless
the ships did sail and, while the famine was not averted, the food saved
thousands of lives that otherwise would have been lost.

Hundreds of Jews began to converge on Evvoia especially after
September 1943 when it became obvious that the Germans were going
to arrest them. As soon as the Athens Jews realized the danger (see
Chapter 6), they began to flee to the mountains or to Evvoia. The latter route via Marathon to Oropos was relatively safe since it was controlled somewhat by 'pirate' clans of Attika. Jews could take a ride with
a friend or in a taxi or even on a bus and make the trip to the coast,
cross over to the island, and find refuge with the help of EAM or ELAS
or independently among the local villages before they could make
arrangements to cross the sea to Turkey. So, Eli Hassid, at age 20, fled
Salonika in March 1943 and with Joseph Hassid went by train to
Athens where they remained until September when they took a bus to
Oropos, crossed to Evvoia and went to the *andartes* in Ano Sateni.
Yomtov Mosheh and several other Jews from Ioannina also crossed
from Oropos to the *andartes* of Eretria in October 1943.[13]

It was soon recognized that a more organized means of escape was
necessary. Contrary to published accounts, however, contact was
apparently initiated by the *andartes* on the island. The report is based
on the interview with Alberto Amarilio (alias 'Aleko'), who had been a
prominent Zionist in Salonika until 1941.[14] Shortly before he left
Greece on 19 April, he was approached by Byron and Mimi, two leaders of the *andartes* on Evvoia, who invited him to a restaurant. They

had heard of his relationship to those who commanded the VIth Corps at Kalyvia and proposed that he pass on their desire to institute relations with the Leftist Party in Palestine of which they had heard much. They passed on their appreciation for the several hundred (actually 200) pairs of boots that 'the Jews sent them,' and requested that the Jews of Turkey be organized to send them money, ammunition, and clothing. Their contact would be Michail Tragonis in the village of Kouste near Çesme. They gave Amarilio half of a 5,000 drachma note to establish contact, but he was unsuccessful in making any arrangements in Izmir and passed on the information and drachma note to the American special envoy, Homer Davis, in Izmir.[15] Davis asked him to make a written report on the situation in Greece and the problems Jews encountered in escaping. The report was also read by A. Barki who worked for the AJDC and Maurice J. de Giaves of the Jewish Agency. According to Ehud Avriel, the Mossad (Organization for Illegal Immigration, a branch of the Hagganah) in early 1944, sent Moshe Agami to Izmir to see Barki who was already engaged in the process of smuggling food and medicines to his brother in Athens.[16] Barki sent Agami to Thomas, the leader of the smugglers, who informed Agami that he was a member of EAM–ELAS.[17] Soon an agreement was concluded whereby the Mossad would pay one gold coin for each Jew that reached Turkey. By the end of the war the escape route had brought over 1,000 Jews to the safety of Turkish shores from which they were sent overland via Syria to Palestine, Sinai, and Egypt. Individuals still attempted to find their own way, and some did not succeed.[18]

How were things organized on Evvoia, the middle portage of the trip to safety? On the island itself Jews had to find accommodation and protection. Amorilio gave a detailed description of the Greek resistance on Evvoia. The VIth *Syntagma* (Regiment) headquartered in Kalyvia had played host to him. It consisted of 5–10 *tagmas* (companies), each with 100–120 men led by a *kapetan*. The subunit of each *tagma* was the *omas* (platoon) with 10–20 men. Each *syntagma* had two kommisars called *politikos* assigned by EAM who directed military matters; they were named Nikita and Dobros. An American liaison group of 12 military men headed by an English captain, 'James,' lived apart from the units.[19] It was the two kommisars, Byron and Mimi, who initiated the idea of arranging supplies, complaining that the British were short supplying them with ammunition in preference to their rival EDES.[20] ELAS, however, had about 100–120,000 men and controlled all the mountains in Greece save for Epirus where EDES was restricted. This information would become public knowledge in Palestine after the arrival of Palestinian journalists with the British 'liberators.'[21] In the meantime it served to forge strong relations that benefited the Jews trying to escape and the survivors in the months immediately follow-ing the retreat of the Germans.

Amarilio was more specific on the individual *andartes* in Evvoia and important political contacts in Athens. Mimi, one of the *andarte* leaders in Evvoia, had responsibility for the boat schedules; he was also quar-termaster with responsibility for supplies and lodging. He had heartfelt sympathy for the Jews and was a confirmed Socialist. His superior was Byron and his subordinate Statis. Janis Angilas, head of the village of Gramatiko, assisted the escape of Jews. His contact was Gheorghios Mavros, a lawyer who was partner in a fabric store with Salomon Kimhi, a staunch support of Venizelos. Mavros was an important polit-ical figure who sympathized with Jews and helped them. Another prominent Venizelist who aided Jews was Galanos (alias Barba) Costa; the police often approached him to exert his influence, since he was an important EAM leader. Aristotelis Coudojumaris (*sic*), director of the Greek Red Cross and a friend of Mavros, also sympathized with and freely helped Jews. The last three were prominent in Athens and had good connections to the British. One of Alchanati's close friends, Karamedzanes, was a central figure in EAM; in September 1943 he organized the flight of some 1,500–2,000 Jews to the mountains.[22] Nico Mitoudi of Salonika was a member of EAM who assisted Jews and pro-vided them with false Greek identification documents so that they could escape from Salonika. Costa Pappas, an important figure in EAM and a former administrative head of the Greek Parliament, aided Jews. Fivos Papachrysanthou owned a large printing house where he printed bank notes for the Greek government. Costa Zavitsanos was an impor-tant figure in EAM who controlled the government purse in Athens. He was sympathetic to Jews and assisted them with Greek Christian iden-tification cards that he obtained from his government contacts. To Amarilio's list we may add Sotiris Papastratis, who was, according to Joseph Lovinger (postwar president of the Jewish Community) head of the partisans assigned to the escape network.[23]

Amarilio was careful to list the individuals on Evvoia who were sympathetic to and helped the Jews, including one, Dedis, who was a central figure in EAM and could be found near Zarkas and Tsikeos. Captain Stellios Hiotis could be trusted to ferry Jews to Turkey; he was a friend of Dr Kyrios, a physician in Vathia. Admiral Jorgios Lembisis, the prewar head of the airforce in Macedonia, was a freemason and helped Jews in Athens.[24] His relative was the lawyer Sotiri Lembisis, a leader of the *andartes* in Evvoia. Their agent was the youth Petraki who escorted Jews from Athens to Evvoia; Petraki was a friend of Moris Saporta. Captain Stamatis ferried Jews from Greece. Contacts who could be hired to assist Jews included: Christo Anatasi[o]u of Evvoia took 2 million drachmas to bring Jews from Athens; a university student named Costa was paid £1 10s to drive each Jew to Marathon; Nico Costopoulos, a captain from Piraeus, ferried Jews to Turkey; and a boat owner named Jani Kukulomatis from Athens could be hired to take Jews to Turkey.

Amarilio's reports give us a sociological profile of the resistance leadership that helps to explain further the difference between the fate of the Jews in Salonika and Athens. In Salonika the Jews were relatively isolated from the rest of the population since their major pursuit was trade. Thus Salonika did not produce many Jewish professionals or intellectuals who could establish relationships with their counterparts in the broader society.[25] In Athens (see Chapter 6), on the contrary, Jews had been pursuing professional careers since the late nineteenth century. The men he denotes as friends of the Jews were Venizelists in Athens, as were their Jewish friends.[26] In Salonika, as we saw earlier, it was lower middle-class Greeks, students, and army veterans who were friends with their social equals. Many were freemasons, and the popularity of this organization among the Greek military, the Church leadership, and Jewish professionals is a subject that demands further research.[27] And finally, the family network that embraced close friends paralleled the general structure of Greek paternalism; this phenomenon was a characteristic of the Athenian Jews who by virtue of education, interests, and language were Jewish counterparts of their fellow Greeks. The importance of EAM in Athens in the rescue and support network cannot be overstressed and has to be examined separately from the KKE attitude toward the Jews noted above (Chapter 1), which was also positive.

Amarilio also supplied the names of local ELAS officials and commanders on Evvoia and a few EDES supporters, although with no mention of their attitude toward the Jews. These included: Byron, the superior of Mimi, who recruited Amarilio to set up a supply with the Hagganah, and Statis, Mimi's subordinate. Nikita and Dobros, political kommisars of *Syntagma* VI; Ernis, leader of the *andartes* in Evangelistra; Costa or Constantin Georgio, who was a courier to Turkey and Egypt; Lucas, an investigating officer for EAM in Tsikios; Michaelis, an *andarte* leader in Limnona; Micos, a pharmaceutical supplier in Athens and member of EDES who helped Greeks flee to Egypt; Mitsos, an *andarte* leader in Gramatiko; and the mysterious Michael Tragounis, the ELAS representative in Turkey.

By the beginning of 1944 the Jewish Affairs – Emigration desk in Jerusalem knew, via the Amarilio report, that Leon Azouli had been appointed by EAM as representative of all the Jewish refugees in Evvoia. Leon had been a member of EAM for over two years by that time and was a logical choice to organize an increasingly burdensome and potentially dangerous situation. If enough Jews were to come to the island and destabilize it, then the Germans might come in force to capture them and punish the local population. There were after all enough collaborators to inform the Germans of the developing situation.[28] An internal report[29] lists the location of a number of Jews on the island. Leon Azouli was located in the village of Yimnon where he was the head of 24 Jews. Isac Chanen (alias 'Sophianos') led 50 Jews. In the villages of Teologos were several Jews from Halkis and in Magula there were 14 Jews. At the *andarte* headquarters in Sateni there were 50 Jews. The report notes that the Rabbi remained in Halkis. It is noteworthy that he does not mention Sarika or name any of the other Jewish *andartes*.

New revelations from the recently declassified OSS files add another chapter to the Evvoia story. At the end of 1942, shortly after the Soviets had sent agents into Greek cities and the British had established their mission in the mountains of Sterea Ellada, the Americans began to look at what options would be available to them in Greece. Most scholars, following wartime British opinion and relying on the domestic American scene, have ignored the American interest in Greece during the war. Italy after all was an ally of the Axis; American troops were in North Africa heading toward Tunisia and preparing for an invasion of Italy. American strategy seemed poised to invade Europe from the south to liberate Rome and from the northwest to liberate Paris. The OSS had a broader vision, however.

The Deputy Director of the OSS was Lieutenant Colonel (later Colonel) Ulius L. Amoss. On June 25, 1942 he sent to Major David K.E. Bruce, Head of OSS Intelligence Section, a 'Primary Blue Print for Creation and Functioning of East European Section's Secret Intelligence.'[30] Amoss followed up on August 11 with a conceptual plan for a Greek Irregular Project that apparently had been the basis for his joining the OSS on December 16, 1941 at the request of William Donovan. Amoss explained the rationale for his plan – to be kept absolutely secret[31] – to Donovan by summarizing a conversation he had with a Professor Carl Haushofer in 1922. According to Amoss,

Haushofer had announced a 'Geo-Politik that affected every civilized person in the world,' and especially the Germans. According to him Greece was the most important of the Balkan States!

Despite the disasters that Greece experienced in the wake of the Asia Minor debacle and the ensuing political, social, and economic catastrophes as well as the threat of a Turkish invasion, Haushofer ranked Greece as highest among the Balkan States followed by Yugoslavia, Turkey, Bulgaria, Romania and Albania. He went on to say:

> The defeat of Greece is temporary. Greece is used to disaster and will turn this one into a blessing. The American Greeks will bring new strength to the mainland; will introduce new skills and trades ... "Old Greeks" will have to step up enterprise. A wave of patriotism will sweep every Greek community in the world.

Money would pour in from Greeks and Philhellenes. There would be new opportunities and new immigration. 'Greece,' he prophesied, 'is important to the future plans of Germany.' Greece was the key to Eastern Europe and the rest of the world through the potential of its commerce, foreign trade, politics, and espionage. Germany would fill Greece with secret agents and force Greece into supporting Germany's future plans.

Well, that had to be one impressive performance! Though Haushofer, according to Amoss, was considered to be a charlatan in the West, nevertheless he was sharp enough to realize the potential of Haushofer's argument; and indeed anyone who analyzed the growth of German influence in Greece during the 1930s would realize the importance the Nazis gave to his vision. Hence Amoss took the opportunity to counter the Haushofer plan under the auspices of the OSS. The first stage would be the Greek Irregular Project headed by Stavros Theofanides, Minister of Mercantile Marine for Greece and a specialist in American affairs, and answerable to Vice Premier Canellopoulos of the Greek Government of Exile in Cairo. The Greek minister in Ankara would collect data and forward it to Theofanides who was based in New York. In ultimate control, however, would be the OSS. The data would come from the worldwide Greek diaspora that was linked by Greek seamen. The Greek colonies from Ethiopia to Romania and from Turkey to Vienna would also be significant, because they blanketed one of the important theaters of the war. Maniadakis, former head of national security for Metaxas and still on the government's payroll, was active in South America. Admiral Canaris of the Abwehr was a 'Greek' serving in the German army who might be persuaded to turn. Amoss's argument for a worldwide net of potential Greek agents totally eclipsed the Nazi fear of the 'Elders of Zion' and the American fear of the 'Communists.' He planned, and even promised, to organize the American Greek community through AHEPA, the ubiquitous Greek fraternity in the United States, and the world wide presence of the Orthodox clergy. Donovan was impressed enough to fund the Greek Irregular Project for six months (January–July 1943) for $300,000. On July 16 he recommended that the project should become regular. Eventually, in addition to its primary military function of gaining intelligence on the mainland, it would be expanded through the War Refugee Board effort to save Jews.

Amoss was soon out of the picture once the project was put on a regular basis, but it was his vision and argument for the project that succeeded in setting up the secret liaison with the British SIS in Cairo that resulted in the development of an important American base on the Turkish coast near Çesme. The base, codenamed Boston, had listening posts set up throughout the Aegean and sponsored missions to the eastern part of Greece and to Crete. It was headed by Major John L. Caskey.[32] Already on July 11, 1942 he (then a captain)had been designated to set up a contact center in Izmir for occupied Greece). His SIS contact was Lieutenant Commander N.C. Rees who headed a base in another bay. The bound volume of Casky's reports of his missions begins with Weekly Report 1 dated 30 December 1943 and continues to 5 January 1944.[33] We shall confine our survey to his contacts with Evvoia in this chapter.

On January 11, Casky reported that the Evvoia *andartes* were unreliable. They were suspicious of the British who had failed to establish a mission among them, but they were willing to work with the Americans. This entry would characterize nearly all of the OSS reports from Greece and would contribute to the friction between the American and British missions. On February 4, a caique returned with 3 Italian soldiers, 4 Jewish refugees, and 35 Greek civilians from Evvoia for recruitment to the Greek military. The caique landed at the British base, a landing that resulted in a change in British policy to accept civilians in the future. On March 3, Captain Trig of the Agios Nikolaos (one of the ten caiques operating the 'caique-ferry' at the time) acceded to the request of the *andartes* to take 26 Jewish refugees to Turkey; however, part-way through the voyage the caique broke down[34] and he was forced to land at Rees' base, codenamed Kioste, and leave the refugees there. Rees protested the intrusion, and after Caskey apologized Rees said that he was 'quite willing when necessary to take care of refugees brought by our caiques and landed unobtrusively on the Chesme peninsula.' Caskey for his part was not annoyed by the delay of one of his caiques for a week 'in order to bring out 40 Jewish refugees, who were undoubtedly milked of their possessions' by local Greek subagents.[35]

Herein lay a fundamental difference between the Americans and the British. The British were annoyed that the Jews had flooded Evvoia with refugees, who bid up the price of caiques in their panic to escape Greece: both phenomena interfered with a prime British directive to rescue British soldiers.[36] It also interfered with British attempts to smuggle their own agents into Greece. This annoyance on the front line (understandable) masked the larger British problem of Arab complaints against Jewish migration to Palestine, which the British had curtailed in their infamous White Paper of 1939. A conference on 29 April, 1944 between Major Caskey, and Colonel Simonds and Maj. Caridia of A Force cleared the air somewhat. At conference

> Col. Simonds stated that the increasing number of Jews who are coming out (partly, no doubt, because they pay big sums privately to the caique captains) are straining relations between A Force and the anti-Semitic Turkish authorities. He regretted on humanitarian grounds to discourage the rescue of Jews, but felt that, for the sake of the principal work, this traffic should not be carried by the secret services now operating. He hoped that a jewish(!) rescue service would be established, make its own arrangements with the Turks, and operate its own caiques.

Caskey summarized the problem he faced and asked Cairo for direction:

> OSS Izmir has long been aware of the dangers to its own work which are inherent in any activity unwelcome to the Turks, and therefore normally steers clear of all rescue and escape operations. Maj. Caskey gave assurance that every effort would be made to avoid embarrassing A Force with Jewish refugees, but pointed out that in the light of recent statements by President Roosevelt and Ambassador Steinhardt it might become increasingly difficult for an American service to avoid giving help to stranded Jews. It was the opinion of Maj. Caskey, as of Lt. Comdr. Rees and others, that the Turks would certainly not authorize the

1 Louis Cohen, ELAS partisan known under the *nom de guerre* 'Kapetan Kronos', Elefsina, October 1944

2 Group of ELAS partisans, Krona, Dervenochoria, Attica, 1944

3 Model platoon of youths, 2nd Division of ELAS, October 1944

4 Louis Cohen on horseback, Mt Parnassos, 17 February 1944

5 Dr Manolis Arouh with fellow partisans in one of their postings

6 Partisan Dr Manolis Arouh in his military uniform

7 Volunteer nurses Ellie Sakki-Decastro and Anna Cohen-Angel of the Greek Red Cross

8 Moisis Matathias with other ELAS partisans

9 Joseph Matsas, Makrakomi, December 1947. Matsas fought in many battles as a member of ELAS and also organized the 'Theatre of the Mountains' for the entertainment of his comrades.

10 Yaakov Arar (Harari) and Captain Peter, Macedonia, 1944

operation of a caique service by Jews for their own rescue work. The problem is knotty, and OSS Izmir would welcome a statement of policy, or a directive from headquarters on this subject.

Caskey's reference to the 'recent statements' by the American president and the US ambassador to Turkey points up a tragedy that affected any warning or aid to the Jews of the former Italian zone. On January 26, 1944 Cordell Hull, the American Secretary of State, sent a circular airgram to all American missions except London, Lisbon, Madrid, Stockholm, Bern and Ankara announcing the formation of the War Refugee Board at the highest level of the American government (Secretaries of State, Treasury and War) 'to take action for the immediate rescue and relief of the Jews of Europe and other victims of enemy persecution.' For some reason that the State Department files from Greece do not explain, this message did not reach the American ambassador in Cairo until March. The Aide-Mémoire to the Royal Hellenic Ministry of Foreign Affairs in Cairo, dated March 16, 1944, mentions only aid and rescue of refugees; there is no mention of Jews. On March 23, Harold Schwartz, Counselor of the Embassy, explains the lack of receipt of the message and the aide-memoire. Hull sent a telegram on March 24 announcing the President's evening radio bulletin warning the Axis and its satellites not to assist 'Hitler's program to exterminate the Jews and other similar groups.' On March 29 the radio statement was given to the Greek government in Cairo and that night the Greek prime minister, Emmanuel Tsouderos, issued a declaration:

> address to all Hellenes the request that they take particular notice of his recommendation that the Allied Balkan peoples help in the rescue and escape to neutral or friendly countries of the Jews now threatened by new and inhuman persecution, or of any other victims of Nazi tyranny.

This declaration was broadcast to Greece on March 31 at 1:15 p.m., 7:30 p.m. and 10:30 p.m.[37]

The Jews of the former Italian zone were arrested on Passover 1944, which fell on the night of March 24/25. The question mutely rises from the grave: why was there a delay of two months between President Roosevelt's executive order and its arrival to his faithful Ambassador Lincoln MacVeagh in Cairo?

A number of agencies (political, military, and civilian) capable of effecting the rescue of large numbers of Jews from Greece were already in place among the British and the Americans. These included ELAS, British, American, and private caique services,[38] and representatives of the American Joint Distribution Committee, UNRRA, the Jewish Agency, and the American diplomatic services in Cairo, Istanbul, and Izmir, along with the hospitality of the Greek consul in Izmir. 'Considering the geographical position of Greece, which is one of the best in occupied Europe, the number of escapes has been very few,' observed Alfred Cohen, Legal Advisor at the Greek Foreign Office on May 31, 1944. Earlier in the month Irving Friedman, in a memorandum dated May 18, noted that 'Since December about 250 Jewish refugees from Evvoia via caiques operated by British navy in conjunction with American military personnel.' It would be better, he continued, if the caiques, which could carry 50-60 people, were more full than the 20 on average transported.[39]

On June 28, Burton Berry, the American Consul General in Istanbul, visited Major Caskey and asked if Caskey could 'do anything to help the Jews.' Caskey replied that he did not have the facilities to do so. Unfortunately he was unaware that Berry was expending considerable effort both in Turkey and in Washington to effect the rescue of Jews in accordance with the directives of the War Refugee Board, and so had little patience for military protocol.[40] The difficulties with the Turks would continue until the Turkish government broke off relations with Germany at the beginning of August 1944. From that time it was free to act openly with the Allies and so some of the problems connected with Jewish refugees were alleviated.[41]

The issues summarized by Alfred Cohen in his report were listed in the memorandum prepared by Henry Hill dated July 5, 1944 for Ambassador MacVeagh to be carried by the latter to the United States which would result in further delays).[42] The extract below gives an appreciation of what happened to the president's call in January 'to take action for the immediate rescue and relief of the Jews of Europe and other victims of enemy persecution.'

Greek Jews – War Refugee Board

The Embassy has reported as to savings, upkeep, possibly using ferry service of Anglo-American Intelligence Services for Greek Jews. State Department has been requested to approach War Department, they in turn to approach British War Office, both to instruct British and American intelligence Services, facilitate departure of Jews from Greece, supply Gold sovereigns in

Greece for the upkeep of Jews in hiding, matter being handled principally by Ambassador Steinhardt.

The problem went much further than the Evvoia–Izmir ferry service, however. It reached up through the various British services as far as London and permeated nearly all British diplomatic stations throughout the Mediterranean theater.[43] Even Rabbi Barzilai's appeal, after he came under the protection of ELAS (see Ch. 6), for funds to assist the resistance reached the highest level and was characteristically responded to in rather cavalier fashion by Churchill.

> This requires careful handling. It is quite possible that rich Jews will pay large sums of money to escape being murdered by the Huns. It is tiresome that this money should get into the hands of E.L.A.S., but why on earth we should go and argue with the United States about it I cannot conceive.... We should take a great responsibility if we prevented the escape of Jews, even if they should be rich Jews. I know it is the modern view that all rich people should be put to death wherever found, but it is a pity that we should take up that attitude at the present time. After all, they have no doubt paid for their liberation so high that in future they will only be poor Jews, and therefore have the ordinary rights of human beings.[44]

Britain had its own agenda, which was to bring the king back to Greece and defeat EAM–ELAS from which it feared a Communist takeover.[45]

The above material points out the divergence in tactics between the British and the American military and the difficulties the military encountered in the face of political pressures by diplomats. The Jews were only the bellwether for such tensions. Britain was reluctant to send supplies to ELAS, which desperately needed shoes, weapons and ammunition. The British would not allow the Americans to interfere with their curtailment of aid to ELAS and OSS Izmir was under orders not to distribute weapons outside its own organization.[46] The higher humanitarian principle that the British invoked reads hollow in the face of unrestricted warfare on German civilians and lack of concern for 'collateral damage' among the slave workers and other prisoners of the Nazis.

Evvoia, given its fortuitous geographical location, emerges from these reports and anecdotes as an important station on the transportation network into and out of Greece. Its mountains and beaches made it virtually impossible for the Germans to control, although they could punish the resistance in occasional sweeps such as in January 1944. It succeeded in protecting its own Jews who sought out *andartiko* aid and in providing refuge for many more who came from the mainland. ELAS even interfered with Allied missions by placing Jewish refugees on their caiques. Jews could be found active in the resistance, in helping their coreligionists to escape to Turkey, and in organizing a new supply line for the *andartes* in Evvoia and central Greece to supplement the British support. The statue to Colonel Mordecai Frizis that stands prominently in Halkis, a legacy of Ioannis Metaxas's respect for his valor and sacrifice during the fight against the Italian invaders, is fitting tribute and a reminder of the contributions of Greek and Palestinian Jews on the island during the war.

NOTES

1. For parallels cf. Ismail Kadare, *Chronicle in Stone* (London, 1987). A similar situation is reported for Ioannina where the mothers of youths who went to the mountains brought them home.
2. She was the daughter of Alberto Carasso who was shot as a hostage on December 30, 1942 with 44 Greek Christians in retaliation for the blowing up of a bridge. His twin brother was shot on May 1, 1944 along with 199 Greek Christians. The two twins are buried respectively in the two mass graves in a Christian cemetery. She later married Yitzhak Mosheh ('Kitsos'] and bore twins. In November 1949 they immigrated to Israel.
3. He was a wartime comrade of Alberto Molho who was shot and wounded by the Germans for trying to escape the forced labor. This friend gave Molho's wound a special treatment to prevent it from healing, because, if it had, the Germans would have excuted him. Molho was sent to Auschwitz in the first transport on March 15, 1943. The friend who came to rescue Alberto was asked to save the family of the other Alberto (Carasso).
4. She identified 'Leonivas' (read 'Leonidas') as secretary for the area; he later became commander. 'Christos' succeeded him. The intellectuals and professionals of Negrita, as elsewhere, contributed to the resistance, especially the teachers.
5. YVS 03/0544. Elsewhere in her 1988 interview, she recalls meeting only one other Jew in the mountains; he was Albert Preznalis of Serres (see Chapter 1). This suggests that the Christian disguises adopted by Jews in the mountains and the false papers supplied by EAM or ELAS were so effective that, unless Jews knew each other personally, there was no way for any individual – participant or scholar – to get an accurate account of the Jewish story in the mountains. For the women's role in EPON see memoirs collected by Altamirano, Fourtouni, and Hart below.
6. Further data on C.K. can be gleaned from her brother Frederic Kakis's memoir *Legacy of Courage. A Holocaust Survival Story in Greece* (Bloomington, IN, 2003). Their mother was an intelligent and independent woman, and the rest of the family was active in the *andartiko*.
7. Her mother and two younger brothers were hiding on nearby Skiathos. The boys were in ELAS's youth movement, EPON. (See Chapter 1.)
8. Interview with Yeti Mitrani, her daughter. The Molho family, whom I interviewed in 1998, in the bookstore in Salonika, also hid out on Skopelos. Neither knew of the other's presence during the war. After the war Molho's son reopened the bookshop and employed Daisy Carasso Mosheh until she emigrated with her family.
9. Constantine Poulos, 'Report on Greece,' Taminent Library, New York University, Box 1, File 39, pp. 21–3 (reprinted with permission of the Taminent archivist). Poulos entered Greece from Turkey via an OSS caique (see below) and wrote a series of articles based on his extensive travels throughout occupied Greece.

10. See now Deborah Renee Altamirano, 'Up in arms: The lives and times of women activists in the World War II Greek Resistance', Ph.D. thesis (University of California at Santa Barbara, March 1993). Altamarino states that up to one-third of the female population was involved in resistance activities.

11. See previous note; Eleni Fourtouni, *Greek Women in Resistance* (New Haven 1985); Janet Hart, *New Voices in the Nation. Women and the Greek Resistance, 1941–1964* (Ithaca, 1996).

12. Other Jewish refugees were debriefed by the American consul, the Jewish Agency, and the predecessors of the Mossad in Istanbul. Still others by a variety of services, including British and American in Palestine and Cairo. Much of this material can be found in the Central Zionist Archives in Jerusalem.

13. Both were interviewed by the author in March 1997. See also Sotiris Papastratis, *Meres tou 1943–1944 sten Euvoia* (Days of 1943–1944 in Evia) (n.p., 1995), pp. 116–23 on the escape of the Jews from Evia and the author's role, for which he was honoured by Yad Vashem. My thanks to his brother Orestis for providing me with a copy of this rare publication.

14. Greece - March 1943 to April 1944, Hagganah Archives, file 14/51, dated 11.6.44, p. 84. He was the legal representative of the Zionists to the Jewish Community in Salonika and treasurer for the community and for the Hirsch Hospital as well as director for the Keren Hayesod in Greece, an impeccable source for the Jewish Agency. In 1941 he left for Athens and from March to December 1943 he served on the ad hoc secret Jewish Counsel to aid Salonikan Jews with Daniel Alchanati, Pepo Benoziliu, and two non-Zionists, Hayyim ben Dubi and Eli Attas. Ben Dubi and Attas were members of the Bnei Brith and possibly maintained relations with Greek Freemasons who later helped Jews to hide and escape.

    Alberto Amarilio escaped with his son Paulos to the mountains where he hid under the protection of ELAS in Kalyvia from September to December 1943 during the initial phase of the German persecution in Athens. He left Greece on 19 April with 62 Jews on a caique that ferried a group of Greeks to Turkey.

15. Davis reported all to Burton Berry, the American consul, who sent informative reports to the State Department where they languished unread until Michael Matsas began to read them for his book *Illusion of Safety* (New York, 1997),.

16. *Open the Gates* cited in Matsas, *Illusion of Safety*, p. 102 where he identifies the contact as Raphael Baki.

17. Thomas was imprisoned by the British in their crackdown on ELAS after the liberation of Greece. He wrote a plaintive letter to the Jewish Agency requesting their intercession with the British that he be deported to Russia where he could continue the fight against the enemy. There is no further data on Thomas in the files I examined.

18. See Matsas, *Illusion of Safety*, pp 102–6 and sources cited in my *Agony of Greek Jewry during World War II* (forthcoming). See sources and discussion in Tuvia Frilling, 'Between Friendly and Hostile Neutrality: Turkey and the Jews during World War II', in *The Last Ottoman Century and Beyond: The Jews in Turkey and the Balkans 1808–1945* (Tel Aviv, 2002), II, pp. 407–16.

19. The American missions to Greece were under the authority of the British insofar as policy was concerned. Greece was 'a British show', as the OSS acknowledged.

20. The OSS mission reports to be discussed below will support this relationship.

21. As a result of his coverage of the Greek liberation Menahem Dorman produced his first book, *Milhemet haezrahim biyavan – Detsember 1944–yanuar 1945* (Tel Aviv, 1945).

22. See Ch. 6. A number of Jews have emphasized their surprise that virtually the whole Jewish community disappeared overnight. Karamedzanes's role and connections in this matter have not been researched to date.

23. See his letter in Matsas, *Illusion of Safety*, pp. 171f. Lovinger and his wife were hidden in Athens by Emmanuel Kothris, former secretary of the Eleftherios Venizelos Youth Organization, who later took him to Evvoia. From the port of Tsakkei he took a caique with Laszlo Velica, the Hungarian ambassador, and his wife to safety.

24. He played host to Salvatore ben Yaish, for whom see Ch. 1.

25. Exceptions of course were to be found among those who held foreign citizenship. These were generally the wealthier merchants and manufacturers or journalists with important ties to the wider community.

26. To complicate matters many Venizelists in Salonika were anti-Jewish.

27. My thanks to the late P. K. Vatikiotis for this observation.

28. According to Eli Hassid, Kapetan Orestes crossed to the island at the beginning of 1944 to

organize Eretria and blow up houses of collaborators. The head of the OSS Mission Stygia to Evvoia described General Orestes, Executive Officer of the 5th Brigade as , 'quite a character – a large edition of Adolph Menjou, resplendent in captured finery – a Brooks quality flannel shirt, gabardine jodpurs, good boots, a sheepskin coat I'd give my eyeteeth for – all set off by a fur cap and a large handlebar moustache ... He had come to Evvoia with fifteen officers and men, all mounted on beautiful horses which they brought over on caiques' (NARA 226/190/2/file 19). During September and October 1944 Hassid took part in fighting near the ferry that crosses to Volos, apparently to harass the German retreat from the island (interview 17 March, 1997).

29. "Greece – up to December 1943/Jewish Affairs – Emigration, Hagganah Archives, File 14/51, dated 4.1.1944. Spelling is preserved as in the document and is based on the Amarilio debriefing.

30. NARA 210/410/04.

31. As far as he was concerned only SIS Cairo could be trusted to keep the secret.

32. Caskey was an archaeologist who would lead a distinguished postwar career alongside Carl Blegen at the University of Cincinnati. His cover in Turkey was as representative of the Lend-Lease Program.

33. NARA 210/277/02.

34. A constant problem for the American caiques that was never resolved. When a report of the Aegean caique Ferrying Service was drawn up, the technical complaint of inefficient and constant breakdowns – of 15 caiques on January 2, 1944, only 2 were fit for service – led to a query to the British in Haifa. Lt. Com. Therin was happy to explain how the British solved the problem. When they began the caique service they converted British Leyland tank engines to maritime use. Major Wallace, the British conversion engineer, was available to explain how to adjust the caique to carry the weight. NARA 210/277/2.

35. Report No. 31 3–9 Aug 44. NARA 210/277/2. Caskey lists German and Italian prisoners brought on his caiques. Other reports indicate the help rendered to the British invasion of Samos.

36. The report of 'Brigand' dated April 7, 1944 (NARA 210/277/4) describes the failure of his mission at the end of September 1943. 'Conditions in Athens were abnormal due to the collapse of Italy, the persecution of the Jews, and internal strife between factions. Prices for caiques were skyhigh and no suitable boats were to be found because Jews were paying large sums for craft of any kind.'

37. NARA 84/2649A/69/848/Greek refugees.

38. Including rumors about a Jewish organization starting up a ferry service with a few caiques; there is even an obscure mention of an Operation Moses to rescue Jews, possibly under US auspices (if not an allusion to Moses Agami's mission). For Palestinian efforts at rescue from Greece via a boat service, see Frilling, 'Between Friendly and Hostile Neutrality.' This was apparently the rescue service noted earlier that the Americans suggested be coordinated or curtailed lest it interfere with a broader rescue effort planned by the United States. He does not mention any Operation Moses. The Palestinian agent in charge of the operation, Mosheh Averbuch (Agami), estimated 2,000–3,000 Jews rescued. Historians more conservatively suggest about 1,000. American Joint Distribution Committee lists of Greek Jews brought to Turkey number less than 1,000.

39. In the last 6 months of 1943 some 280 Jews were rescued by the Palestinian-ELAS boat service (see previous note) according to Menahem Bader who reported on December 12 1943 to the Executive Committee of the Histadrut on efforts organized from Istanbul. There were 3 other boats on the way to Evvoia and some 600 Jews waiting for them. The problem was the willingness of the Mandatory government to award them certificates to enter Palestine as Jews and even the difficulties involved in having them registered as refugees. See extracts in Yosef Ben, *Greek Jewry in the Holocaust and the Resistance 1941–1944* (Tel Aviv, 1985), pp. 114f and discussion in Frilling, 'Between Friendly and Hostile Neutrality.' To put the Jewish figures in perspective, we should look at the broader relief problem that the British faced. The multitudes of Orthodox Greeks who reached Cyprus via British warships and the Middle East via Turkey were set up in a series of camps that eventually became part of the extended War Relief administered by MERRA (superseded by UNRRA). A memorandum on the foreign relief and rehabilitation operation dated July 26, 1943 lists 12,695 Greek refugees as of April 8, 1943 (NARA 59/1410/2/Greece DPs). After the September 1943 British invasion of the Dodecanesos islands over 12,000 Greeks abandoned the islands for Cyprus and a new

camp in Gaza. By December the British were planning to build 50 caiques in Haifa for relief services. This idea was proposed by Major Baker (Istanbul), Sidney Simonds (British Embassy commercial attache) and Stavros Theophanides (Greek Minister of Merchant Marine). NARA 84/2649A/61.

40. Berry's story has still to be told. Matsas, *Illusion of Safety*, was the first to point out his importance, although he was unaware of the broader net that extended to Ambassador Lincoln MacVeagh in Cairo and thence to the War Refugee Board in Washington, which reported directly to President Roosevelt.

41. See Frilling, 'Between Friendly and Hostile Neutrality' for a summary of the Turkish difficulties.

42. NARA 84/2649A/62/ folder 123. For local British station reports, see P. R.O. Kew. HS 5/351, 24 July 1944, 22 July 1944, 17 August 1944.

43. See Frilling, 'Between Friendly and Hostile Neutrality,' pp. 407–16.

44. Letter to Foreign Secretary from 10 Downing Steet dated 14.7.44 (FO 371/43689/137459); file contains further discussions about Rabbi Barzilai's call for aid and diplomatic notes to Cairo for consultation with the Greek government there. The discussion was prompted by Ambassador Leeper's call for guidance; the latter ignores the Jews in his memoir *When Greek Meets Greek* (London, 1950). See further *Agony of Greek Jewry*, ch. 9.

45. A report on the Activity of the KKE in Karistos, Evvoia, supported by EAM–ELAS and dated 5-10-44 indicates that there was substance to this fear. Collaborators were executed, property confiscated, and 'all government bureaus were abolished and their own authorities installed.' NARA 226/190/2.

46. See Caskey report December 13, 1944. NARA 210/277/4. This was contrary to British policy, which supplied Tito in Yugoslavia with huge amounts of materiel. It also did not acknowledge the various forms of assistance that Palestinian Jews rendered the British war effort in the Balkans and in Palestine.

4

Kapetan Makkabaios: Honor Regained

Sterea Ellada, or central Greece, comprises the area south of Mount Olympus, east of the mountains of Epirus, and north of Attika. It is mountainous and interspersed with many valleys. The coast road snakes northward paralleling the island of Euboea (Evvoia). It is perfect guerrilla country to retire to following attacks on German convoys and raids on the flat country. Already in 1941 independent bands of klephts and demobilized Greek and Imperial soldiers were forming in the mountains subject to their respective *kapetans*. The most important band in central Greece was that of Aris Velouchiotis, a recanted Communist who went to the hills to regain his honor.[1] It was his band that joined with Napoleon Zervas of EDES in the successful British attack on the Gorgopotomos Bridge on November 25, 1942.[2]

Soon the Communists, under the banner of EAM, began to organize the fledgling resistance movement whose fighting arm was called ELAS.[3] Although an ELAS central committee had been formed in February 1942, it was not before spring of 1943 that a three-man general staff was appointed, consisting of Stephen Serafis as military commander, Aris Veluchiotis as *kapetan* and Andreas Tsimas as *politikos*. Intermittent internecine war raged in the mountains between ELAS and EDES. The British supported EDES for Zervas's ostensible royalist sentiments (he and his band were mostly Venizelist Republican officers, but he was quick to pronounce the right line for his benefactors). ELAS, on the other hand, was held in suspicion by the British (although American observers supported their democratic revolution), and they kept a tight rein on ELAS supplies of weapons and equipment.

The ELAS leader in Sterea Ellada was Colonel Dimitrios Dimitriou, known during the war as 'Nikiforos'. He had previously served as a line officer under Colonel Mordecai Frizis on the Albanian front and remained in the mountains after the surrender. He is a prime source for the careers of a number of Jewish *andartes* who fought with him. Indeed their loyalty to him persevered even during the persecution of former resistance fighters after the war.[4] Two of the men from his headquarters' staff are now in Israel. One was repatriated after a deal in which he renounced his Greek citizenship in lieu of continued imprisonment, one of the few *andartes* who managed to avoid the continued incarceration that plagued them throughout the 1950s and 1960s. In Israel certain authorities informed them and other Greeks who came under the same circumstances that they should keep a low profile. Both were reluctant to be further interviewed; one had agreed to be debriefed at Yad Vashem, however, and the other only recently published his story for the historical record.

Colonel Dimitriou recalled appreciably a number of his Jewish fighters. Their continued loyalty was manifested through their hiding him in Salonika after the war. Several of them had already become legendary among Greek Jews even during the war, in particular those who had died and therefore did not present any political problem. It is axiomatic in Greek tradition since Homer that all heroes are dead heroes. Not all of the heroic figures recalled by this *andarte* chief, however, were killed during the occupation.

The hero most often recalled is Robert Mitranis. As with a number of Jews in the earlier stages of the resistance, he escaped from a forced labor camp. This one was at Kiphisohori (near Loukarida on the slopes of Mount Parnassos); he had been sent there by the Germans to repair the railroad line shortly after the notorious Sabbath registration day in Salonika (July 11, 1942) when some 9,000 Jewish males were harassed, persecuted, and registered for forced labor. Born in Serres in eastern Macedonia – his father was a well-known physician who was killed in Auschwitz, Robert was still a medical student at the beginning of the war. He was assigned to *andartiko* headquarters to set up a medical facility where he was to earn his resistance sobriquet 'Hippokrates'. Later he became the doctor of the first battalion of ELAS. As with other Jewish doctors he also fought and so was available on the front line to tend to those wounded in action.

On January 5, 1944 his unit fell into a German ambush at Agia Triada (between the villages of Kaloskopi and Pavliana between Mount Giona and Mount Itis), and 30 men were killed, decimating the First Company. Robert Mitranis, although wounded several times, died attempting to rescue his commander Kalias, who also had been wounded.[5] Their overall immediate commander, singled out several other Jews (their *andartiko* names were David and Benjamin) for their bravery during battle.[6] All 30 casualties (including 2 Soviet POWS whom the *andartes* had rescued from the Germans) lie buried in a common grave, their names commemorated on the marble stela that marks the site of that battle.

A second doctor recalled by Colonel Dimitriou was Albert Cohen, known as 'Vladimir' to his fellow fighters. He joined V/34 Battalion along with Dr Manolis Arukh in September 1943 during the period when many Jews left Athens due to the Italian surrender and the subsequent German occupation. After the battle of Arahova (near Delphi), they were able to set up a mobile hospital with the large tents that were captured. Albert Cohen was on the front line at the Battle of Dervenohori (near Paratina) and at numerous other battles where he could attend directly to the wounded. According to his commander he is still honored among the *andartiko* veterans of Parnassos.

Dr Manolis (Emmanuel) Arukh was chief medical officer for V/34 Battalion, which quickly gained the reputation as the best medical unit in Sterea Ellada, not only among the *andartes* but also among the mountain populace that frequented the hospital. He also fought bravely with his unit in the field. From January 1944 he served as medical officer with 34/2 Battalion. In August 1944 he was transferred to the headquarters of the Second Brigade where he served until demobilization.

Other Jewish fighters recalled by Colonel Dimitriou include two brothers from Xanthi, Louis Cohen, alias 'Kronos', and his 16-year-old younger brother Yitshak, both active and brave fighters. 'Kronos' was, in addition, assigned to supply where he performed miracles according to his commander. His polyglot skills made him invaluable in interrogating Italian and German prisoners and in liaison with the BLOs from the Allied missions among the *andartes*. Louis received commendations from his commander and Dimitrios Arvenitis (army officer), as well as the approbation of his fellow fighters and denizens in the regions of Parnassos–Giona–Iti for his actions during the Battle of Karoutes on August 5, 1944 in which he was wounded. His brother Yitshak was also commended for his bravery, and is remembered by his fellow fighters as 'Kronaki' (Little Kronos). Other Jewish *andartes* under the command of Dimitriou were Morris Yeshurum, who served from October 1943, Yomtov Moshe (Malias), and Salvator Bakolas, who came to his command from Evvoia.[7]

Colonel Dimitriou particularly recalls two Jewish *andartes* for their bravery and service. Both have left a written record of their exploits to add to his commendation: David Broudo and Ido Shimshi (Kapetan Makkabaios). Both Broudo and Dr Cohen assisted their former commander after the demobilization of ELAS (February 12, 1945). Colonel Dimitriou met with Dr Cohen in Kastoria in October 1945 while he was on the run from the government. Cohen gave him the gold Napoleons that his parents had hidden before they were sent to their deaths in Auschwitz. They met again later in Salonika where he was practicing, and Dr Cohen treated his wife for pneumonia and supported them with food, medicine, and money. Broudo was less fortunate. When he met with his commander in Salonika, he offered him a hiding place at his home: all that was left of the Broudo clan by then was him and his brother; the rest were killed in Auschwitz. Broudo offered to go to Central Greece to learn about Dimitriou's family in Lamia and Parnassos. On his way back to Salonika, Broudo was denounced as a former *andarte* and turned into the police at Levadia. He was later sentenced to 25 years, of which he served 10, before being allowed to leave for Israel where he experienced further the vicissitudes that have embittered him. A look at the figures may help to clarify the hostility toward Jews in Salonika during 1945 and their reception in Israel in subsequent years. In May, of the 800 Jews in the city 200 were identified as ELASites under Communist leadership. They sent their request to immigrate into Palestine since they still feared being drafted into the Greek army.[8]

David Broudo escaped from the German forced labor camp with Robert Mitranis and so both became the first Jews to join 'Nikiforos'. Broudo was assigned to supply, which was more dangerous even than the many battles in which he also aggressively took part. Supplies were gathered from Italian and German camps and transports in the eastern and central zones of Sterea Ellada. When necessary he called up local members of EAM–ELAS for assistance (cf. Kapetan Kitsos in Chapter 2); however, mostly he worked alone and his exploits assumed legendary proportions among *andartes* and civilians alike.[9]

Last, but not least, 'Nikiforos' recalls Kapetan Makkabaios who served with Battalion V, which later became the II Division, and how he helped him when he arrived in Salonika. As to how he earned his *nom de guerre*, that story comes from the memoir of 'Makkabaios' which he published only in 1997, a decade after his wartime exploits were made public and he was honored.[10]

Into or Ido[11] Shimshi was born in Salonika in 1922 to a traditional family in which Judeo-Spanish was the mother tongue. He learned French at the Alliance Israélite Universelle school and later Italian at the Umberto Primo Commercial School, and good Greek in the church playground. Modest even as a youth, he asked his father why he prepared a lavish bar mitzvah for him. 'My son, a bar-mitzvah occurs only once in life; marriage ... perhaps twice.' During the famine of the occupation he joined the Union of Secretaries and soon was secretary and assistant to the head of the Union of Legal Secretaries.

After July 11, 1942 he was sent to forced labor at the chrome mines in Vavdos, Chalkidiki.[12] Fed up with this torture,[13] he joined several Christians and escaped from the camp. He returned to Salonika, but it was difficult to hide; the Germans were looking for him and the deportations were in process. In April 1943 his friend Constantinos Rigas hid him but he was caught by the Germans and put in the Baron Hirsch ghetto. From there he was drafted to forced labor as part of the contingent of 1,500 men sent to Thebes to repair the railroad. The conditions were even worse than in Vavdos: the sick were taken away and shot, others were shot in reprisal for escapes, the German and Ukrainian guards were sadists. In August 1943 he escaped, the day before the survivors were sent back to Salonika and from there to Auschwitz, the last transport from that decimated community.

After various adventures and considerable help from villagers and a priest, he arrived at *andartiko* headquarters, weighing in at 35 kilos. One day an *andarte* returned to camp and proudly announced he had found an accordion; however, it turned out to be a typewriter, and since Shimshi had office experience, he became the secretary of V/34. At that period, he notes, the resistance group comprised mainly peasants, refugees including demobilized soldiers and a few officers, and a handful of Jews. For every three *andartes* there was but one gun, and Shimshi recalls that he went to his first ambush against the Italians unarmed.

In early September Italy surrendered to the Allies and their zone of occupation was overrun by the Germans.[14] Since Shimshi was fluent in Italian he was sent to a junction (Kyriakoki or Aritera) to recruit retreating Italian soldiers to the *andartiko*. At his first attempt he succeeded in recruiting an armed group along with their vehicle loaded with weapons. Another incident made him a live hero. Disguised as a Greek civilian, and armed with a pistol, he joined the local villagers who had stopped a commercial truck. When he began his recruiting speech, one of the soldiers pulled out a grenade, but Shimshi drew his gun and shot him in the hand. They then took the truck back to headquarters. However, it was too heavily loaded with booty, so all the locals had to come out to fix the road and then push the vehicle so that it could reach the mountains. When the truck arrived the *andartes* were all called out to hear the story of this great success. Then the commander addressed Shimshi:

> You are of the nation from which issued the Makkabee heroes. I know that in the past the Makkabees fought against us. In this bold deed which you have done this day you proved that you are

a descendant of those Makkabee heroes of your people. Therefore, from this day your *nom de guerre* shall be called "Makkabaios".' And so it was, from that day on that was how he was known among the *andartes*.[15]

Shimshi's next exploit was to meet with Rabbi Barzilai who had been smuggled out of Athens by EAM–ELAS with the help of Archbishop Damaskinos at the end of September 1943.[16] On the out-skirts of Athens he met a car with a Red Cross Symbol on it. Out stepped the Rabbi, clean-shaven and dressed like a Greek merchant with the identity of Vasilis Mariolis, and his wife. 'Makkabaios' received the guests (who also included several journalists and a dentist) from their guide and protector Thanasis and then turned to address the rabbi in Spanish. That seemed to shock the rabbi, although Shimshi was not the first Jew involved in his escape, as we shall see later. Requisitioning several mules, the party set off to headquarters, care-fully avoiding German search and destroy parties on the way. They arrived safely and were turned over to 'Nikiforos'. The Germans meanwhile went to the village of Kapareli and burned it.

Shimshi remained modest: 'I was not a hero, but I was a talented office administrator.' At headquarters, his commander was 'Orestis' (Andreas Moundrihas), and he happily recalls serving alongside Yannis Ourpanouras, a medical student whose father was head of the Physicians Union in Athens and Postolos Sandas, the journalist, who had climbed to the Acropolis with his friend (Gilesus Tipes) and pulled down the swastika; they then fled to the mountains where they were drawn to the magnetic personality of 'Orestis'.

After liberation, Shimshi returned to Salonika and assisted with the reorganization of the community. Tension was high in the city, espe-cially for the handful of Jews who returned from the mountains and the concentration camps. Squatters and collaborators were unwilling to return property to the destitute Jews; at the same time the government intensified its persecution of the Left. So in 1950 he left for Israel where former *andartes* were supposedly safe from the Greek government. In Israel, however, he was warned shortly after arrival to keep a low pro-file, as were many other former members of the *andartiko* considered potentially dangerous because of the communist reputation of ELAS. Then in 1986 he was invited to an international quiz in Jerusalem about the wartime resistance – one of the questions was about Kapetan Makkabaios. This was the first time his wartime experiences were made public and his identity as Kapetan Makkabaios revealed.

NOTES

1. That is he had signed one of the declarations that Maniadakis exacted from Communists in lieu of further imprisonment or internal exile. Such declarations resulted in expulsion from the Party.
2. See my *Agony of Greek Jewry during World War II* (forthcoming), Ch. 8 for details. Brigadier Edmund Myers, coincidentally of Jewish origin and a career officer, was drafted from the War College in Haifa to lead the mission. See his *Greek Entanglement* (London, 1955).
3. The similarity between ELAS and Ellas (= Greece) was deliberate and confused even literate Greeks.
4. His report, 'Jews in the National Resistance,' can be found in Greek in *Xronika* (January, 1989); in Hebrew in *Apirion* 50 (1997), pp. 8–10; and a summary in English in Michael Matsas, *Illusion of Safety* (New York, 1997), pp. 320–22.
5. One of many witnesses was Zak Behar cited in Miriam Novitch, *Le passage des barbares*, p. 68. Mitrani is identified in other sources as serving in Regiment 13, Company 36 along with 50 Jews from Salonika and Athens.
6. Two of them are identified by Yosef Ben as David Rousso and David Hacohen.
7. Interview with Yomtov Moshe on March 17, 1997 in Tel Aviv. He and Salvator Bakolas were from Ioannina but had joined the *andartiko* in Eretria. See Ch. 5 n. 16 for his story and further details on the Ioannina contingent with 'Nikiforos' who was unaware of their provenance.
8. CZA, S6/4571.
9. He recounts some of his and Albert (Robert) Mitrani's exploits in David Rekanti (ed.), *Zikharon Saloniki* (Tel Aviv, 1971/2), Vol. 2, pp. 565–8.
10. In *Apirion* 50(1997), pp. 11—17 (in Hebrew).
11. So spelled in Greek and pronounced that way. The 'nt' in Greek also represents the sound 'd' (the Greek 'delta' is pronounced as a 'th') and so the name is also voiced as Ido. (Cf. Semitic Adon (lord); Greek Adonis – Anthonis (Anthony, Anton, etc.) This name is recorded as Iddo in Josephus, although I am not sure whether anyone in the Jewish community was aware of this coincidence. More likely the Iddo of Ezra 8, 17 was better known.
12. Other labor sites include Asopos, Thebes, Karara (?), Lianokaladi (?), Larissa, etc.
13. Song of the Salonikan forced laborers: En Vavdos mos karearon / para etsos esforsados / El couero mo lo moundaron / ya estamos atemados / Palas martios i kasmas / tsapas iarabas (They took us to Vavdos for forced labor, They gave us suffering and torture, we passed the limit of tiredness and toil. About us, amidst the running, are many tools: hammers, axes, shovels, and wheelbarrows).
14. For their cruel fate at the hands of the Germans, see Richard Lamb, *War in Italy 1943–1945. A Brutal Story* (New York, 1996), Ch. 8. The Pinerolo Division commanded by General Infante defected to the Allies. Even so tensions remained high between them and the Greeks. In October, the division was disarmed and incarcerated by ELAS (pp. 152 f.). The exploit to be described shows how uncertain was the paper alliance.
15. Since the Greek *andartes* usually took the names of national heroes from their own history, it is a fitting gesture that Shimshi was given one from his own ancestors; I have not found another such name among Jewish *andartes* (with the exception of Dora Bourla's 'Tarzan').
16. See Ch. 6 for details on the Athenian prolegomenon to this story.

5

ELAS: Warriors and Enablers

ELAS eventually emerged as the dominant resistance group in Greece. However, it came late to the scene and had to contend for territory and recruits with various organized and disorganized bands that reflected everything from klephtic thieves to military that refused to surrender and the more dangerous alternative of political ideologies that proliferated in Greece. By the end of 1942 a British Mission had already successfully established itself in the mountains and at the beginning of 1943 the OSS was mobilizing its base in Turkey alongside various British (SO, SI and MO) services. The Allied role was to assist the development of the resistance in Greece, and in the case of the British to try and ward off the civil war brewing between EDES and ELAS.

The British were aware of the Communist-Royalist conflict in the Balkans through Fitzroy MacLean, their liaison to Tito. They were willing to give Tito free reign, however, based on an understanding with Stalin about the future disposition of the Balkans. According to that agreement (formalized 9 October 1944), Greece was to remain in the British orbit. This gentlemen's agreement, despite all the sentiment about loyalty to King George who had brought Greece into the war when Britain stood alone and battered during the Battle of Britain and had inflicted the first defeat on the invincible Axis, was to determine the British attitude toward EAM–ELAS. EAM never quite fathomed the different attitude and support of the British to the resistance movements in the Balkans. Most on the Left eventually simplified the issue by claiming that the British wanted to control Greece after the war and was willing to put monarcho-fascists and collaborators in power to do so. Unfortunately there is some merit to this point of view.

Among the few Jews who were Communists – and there were no Jews in the higher echelons of the KKE who had been to school in Moscow – we find street level organizers like Yitshak Mosheh, Joseph Gattegno, Mosheh Bourlas, and Rosa Cohen, or a Member of Parliament like Zhak Ventura. Most of the Jews who joined EAM, ELAS, or EPON were young Socialists or happenstance volunteers and recruits. For those few Jews of Salonika who chose to escape to the mountains to fight, their attachment to ELAS was fortuitous. In many cases it depended on the recruiting agent. Later, when the Jews of central and southern Greece went to the mountains, EAM assisted them in their flight. ELAS was already paramount and organized, if not equipped, to fit volunteers into its organization in whatever capacity they were willing to serve.

Abraham Arditi's memoir summarizes the problems and illustrates the special role of Jews (though never acknowledged qua Jews) in the mountains. Recruiters from ELAS and EKKA ('monarchists' as the latter were perceived) flooded Salonika, seeking the masses from the Jewish and other poor quarters.[1] Arditi and his friend Abraham Sciaki discussed the options for a long time before finally deciding to join. However, his friend failed to show in the end, so Arditi accompanied two others to the end of the tramway and met 14 other Jews and the *andarte* guide who directed them to an EKKA officer. They boarded a train filled with Italian soldiers and, after a few stops, were met by Greek contacts. After a few rough nights travel, most of them, exhausted from the preceding six months' malnutrition, returned to Salonika.

The four Jews who were left were hidden and fed in the villages for several weeks. When the *andartes* arrived, Arditi was chosen to be the leader's (Papadopoulos) secretary since he was fluent in Greek(!); one of Arditi's tasks was to tutor Papadopoulos's two children. On their way to the mountains, they stopped at a monastery, many of which actively supported the *andartes* with food and refuge. He recalls the friendship of the villagers who 'used to invite me to all the village parties and even the priest would debate with me for long hours about religion.' One day ELAS units attacked the camp. Arditi refused to join the rather bloody internecine Greek battle and was captured along with a doctor from Cairo.

Arditi was taken to the mountains above Vermion 'where there were many partisans both Christians and Jews.' A Jewish *andarte* advised him to tell the truth, and, after having established his credentials, he was given a typewriter and told to translate French and Italian documents into Greek. Soon he was given officer rank and produced, as part of his duties, a newspaper in Greek for ELAS Regiment 50.[2] When he heard about the deportations from Salonika, he asked for permission to return home, but in Salonika a Greek Christian friend warned him to leave since he could do nothing. Moreover, he added, the young men had sworn (!) not to abandon their families and they considered anyone who fled to the mountains to be a traitor. Finally the friend told him his family had been deported, so Arditi returned to his unit.[3]

After the collapse of Italy in September 1943 the Jewish response in Thessaly was opposite to what occurred in Salonika. There, whole communities transferred to the mountains under the protection of the *andartes*. Esther Yahbes of Larissa recorded her story of life in the male-empty village of Mousala. All the able-bodied men had been recruited into the resistance, and the young Jewish boys and girls who found refuge with their families served in various assignments. About ten Jewish families from Larissa were in the village. By then EAM had completely organized the area, collectivized food distribution for the families of fighters and among the villages, and provided housing and false identification cards for the refugees. Esther recalled that there were many more *andartisses* in the village of Douganis as opposed to the village of Tirnavos at the base of Mount Olympus where she later was hidden. The Germans in the neighboring village of Kazaklar used to swim and bathe in the river that flowed by her village. One day the *andartes* ambushed them and killed 30. All those able to move went up the mountain in anticipation of the reprisal, which would have wiped out the village population. ELAS found them and brought them all to another village.[4]

Albert Yahbes also took refuge in the village of Douganis with his family. Born in Kavalla, he escaped to the Italian zone and joined the *andartiko* along with his uncle and brother-in-law.[5] During the autumn of 1943, when German units came to the villages to requisition food, Albert, who spoke a number of languages, accompanied them. His job was to delay and prevaricate in French and Italian in hope of deterring the Germans from taking the food; later he reported to the *andartes* what had transpired. While in the mountains he helped explain the *andartiko* mission to the villagers and to the Jews and recruited the young men who served mainly as reserves until called up for action by the leaders. The ELAS units of Olympus were in his opinion the best in the *andartiko*, and they had responsibility to attack the main communication roads and rails that crisscrossed central Greece. Albert participated in the Battle of Karyes (below), and later mourned his friends from Larissa whose pictures he found among the Jews shot by the S.S. before the ambush.[6]

Logistics were extremely important for the *andartes*, who had to have the support of the population to survive in the high mountains. We have seen that some *andartes* from each unit were assigned to raid German stores. Others organized the local villages in various cooperatives so that the supply of food could be regular. Lazarus or Eliezer Azaria of Karditsa joined ETA in his area and used his skills as an agriculture expert – as late as 1942–3 he worked for the Bank of Agriculture in Karditsa – to effect a continuous supply of food to the *andartes*. Eventually he became chief of ETA in Thessaly.[7]

Another translator was the father of Yitshak Harari of Kastoria. A middleman for the distribution of village produce to the city, he lost his income when the Germans prohibited movement of foodstuffs. He took his family to the mountains where he was recruited by the *andartes*. His knowledge of English and, more important, his familiarity with the mountain roads, was sufficient to assign him to the British Mission. He remained the only Jew with these *andartes*, guiding the British and procuring supplies from the local villagers for them. Meanwhile his wife and son Yitshak survived on the minimal allotments to families of fighters. Yitshak and his older sister had to walk twice a month to a village some 25 kilometers distant to receive their quota of wheat. He recalls that the wolves were big and the snow deep; he was 13 at the time.[8] After their village was burned twice by the Germans (and their hostess nearly died trying to rescue his mother's sewing machine), the British began to drop supplies. Yitshak became a runner conveying messages from village to village.[9]

In the autumn of 1943 Shealtiel Gattegno walked for 4 nights in a group of 35 recruits through the hills of Thessaly. When they arrived in camp they found about 300 *andartes*, including 75 Jews, poorly armed with Turkish rifles. Soon the British began their missions to drop weapons and ammunition so the *andartes* could blow up bridges and destroy railroad tracks. Gattegno cites the bravery of Dick Benveniste and Zhak Katan.[10]

Marko Carasso, brother of Daisy (see Chapter 3) and son of Alberto, escaped from Salonika in spring 1943 and became an *andarte*. Cited for his bravery in the battle Regiment 16 fought against the *komitatzes*[11] near Kastoria, he was chosen for the Reserve Officers Training School established on September 1, 1943 at ELAS general headquarters.[12] Bitter after the death of his father who had been shot by the Germans during one of their frequent reprisal executions of hostages (see Chapter 2), the resistance gave him his father's watch and said that his father's last words were for him to go to the mountains and fight the Germans. Every battle Marco fought was, according to his sister, to avenge his father. He died during an attack on a train at Muharrem Hani in July 1944.[13]

Other officers in ELAS included Lieutenant Samuel Eskenazi from Larissa, a decorated veteran of the Albanian war; he commanded a company in Regiment 54 and was killed at Kalas Straits.[14] Lieutenant

Yohannas Hadjis of Arta (*nom de guerre* 'Skoufas') already had the rank of Second Lieutenant from his Albanian service. As a First Lieutenant he died leading his company in the successful attack on German units in Amphissa. Joseph Matsas recalls the *klephtiko* lyrics of Hadjis' men: 'Skoufas is going to war along with brave andartes.' The *kastro* of Amphissa is still covered with 1940s slogans.[15]

An eyewitness to the Amphissa episode, Yomtov Mosheh of Ioannina, joined the *andartiko* in Eretria, and two months later crossed to the mainland where his group (of Jews from Ioannina) met 'Makkabaios' (Ido Shimshi) and accompanied Kapetan 'Xronos' to Athens (Psychiko) on December 6, 1944. While with 'Xronos', Mosheh served as aid to Dr Emanuel Arukh. Mosheh and his friends[16] took part in the ambush of German units at Amphissa on February 2, 1944 and then his company retired to the village of Karoutes to rest for a few days. Mosheh took part in the subsequent battle with the Germans on July 1, 1944 in which both sides suffered heavy casualties. He provides a unique testimony that clarifies the tragic end of 'Skoufas', who he avers was killed after he was captured

A few weeks later the Germans mounted a major attack against the *andartes* in Karoutes.[17] The enemy force of 320 camped in the midst of an ELAS 11/34 ambush and was decimated. Only one escaped and he was later captured; the *andartes* suffered 30 dead. Mosheh visited his wounded comrades, his nephew Shlomo Matsil, Viktor Batis, Salvator Bakola, and others, in the *andarte* hospital at Pentsayou(?). His last partisan memory was to recount their joy at successfully attacking the last enemy trains that left Athens.[18]

Jews fought among fellow Greeks throughout the mountain war.[19] Still, there is one battle that stands out as a special Jewish action, at least in the memory of Greek Jews. The story of the ambush at Karyes on May 6, 1944 is dryly listed in the official roster of ELAS actions as follows:

> 6 May. A column of 600 Germans advanced into the southern Olympus district, fell into a 10th division ambush and was decimated. German dead 150, wounded 150, prisoners 18. Booty: 12 heavy machine-guns, 25 Steyrs, 80 rifles, 20 pistols and a large quantity of ammunition. ELAS dead 8, wounded 12.[20]

The actual story is somewhat more dramatic. The Germans headquartered in Larissa had heard of a group of 12 Jewish families from the town who were hiding at Kalyvia tou Handjiara. An SS battalion was dispatched to arrest them, which it did, and then it set fire to the site. Meanwhile, Lieutenant Marko Carasso and several other platoons heard of the Jews' arrest and set up an ambush which caught the column as it passed through a deep ravine. Joseph Matsas, who researched this incident, counted 230 German dead and 14 prisoners, including the officer in command and his interpreter. The Jews were saved.[21] This is the only recorded incident of a specific military action undertaken on behalf of Jews by Jews or the resistance.

In addition to their struggle against the occupation, EAM–ELAS was at the same time attempting to institute a 'laokratic' or people's revolution in the mountains. While it is not incorrect to compare this with Tito's people's revolution in Yugoslavia, it is somewhat misleading since the parties of the Left in Greece still had a strong voice, and many of their leaders and supporters were active in the resistance and in the attempt to bring the mountain villages into the modern world.

Max Varon illuminates his role in EAM's attempt to counteract the black market that pervaded Greece. True, the black market was the only functioning local economy during the first year of occupation when the German army stripped Greece of nearly all its edible food-stuffs and the British blockade compounded the ensuing famine. But the Germans eventually organized Rumanian wheat shipments and also negotiated a deal with the British via the ICRC that allowed Swedish ships to bring in Turkish wheat (and British agents). People remained hungry, however, and the German policy to live off the land exacerbated the dearth of food.[22]

Max Varon escaped (via a small boat) from his home in Bulgarian-occupied Kavalla and fled to Salonika along with tens of thousands of Thracian and Macedonian Greeks. Salonika was a little better, but, when in 1942 the Germans began their persecution of the Jews there, he went to Katerini to try for a train to Athens or at least the Italian zone. The trains were full of German troops so he walked to the end of the German zone and took a caique to Volos and then proceeded to Athens. When the Germans took over Athens and Jews could no longer circulate freely, he was helped to escape by a merchant who worked with agricultural organizations; he sent him to the village of Elasson on Mount Olympus. There Varon became director of an agricultural collective for the 52 villages of Olympus. The Germans prohibited inter-village trade in food-stuffs and periodically came to collect their arbitrary quota. This led to surpluses and shortages of various foodstuffs in different villages: grain in one, cheese in another, oil in a third, etc. Under such circumstances the black market flourished for any normal transaction.

The Organization of Agricultural Institutions in Greece arranged with the Germans to transfer goods from villages to the city. In light of the inane rate of inflation, city workers preferred payment in food; this led to fierce competition with the black market.[23] The surplus 'profit' for the organization from the exchange was funneled to the *andartes*. The resistance was quick to capitalize on this exchange network to transfer weapons and disburse propaganda. The wealthier merchants and industrialists, however, looked with not a little disfavor on this folk movement. So Varon was instructed to engage in 'public relations'. He traveled throughout the region to persuade the villagers to support the organization and not sell their food individually. This was, he explained, to their advantage since the black market only exploited them. He stressed that there was no political intent behind the organization, rather the Communist Party(!) and EAM were working for their own good. What did he know about the KKE's ultimate intentions? As for EAM it was nothing more than the umbrella for all such actions, including the agricultural collective, among the Greek people! The important thing was to organize the Greek people against the Nazis. Periodically, ELAS inspected the villages to check on any civil friction that would have abetted German attempts to incite fratricidal division. Once the patriarch of a family accepted the nonpolitical nature of the collective and supported it, then his sons were free to join the *andartiko*. In any case, the boys had to disappear from the village since the Germans collected them for forced labor in Greece or Germany or put them in jail to keep them out of the resistance. Those who went to the mountains were able to maintain contact with their families and bring supplies to their *synagonistes*. Max Varon kept his false identification card with the name Michael Vyronis until he left the mountains.[24]

During 1943 and 1944 the mission of ELAS units was divided between unifying support in the mountains under ELAS control and the Allied plans to use Greece as a feint for Allied operations in Italy. The story is difficult to disentangle from the postwar apologies and polemics of both sides.[25] It is true that ELAS was used to further the social and political revolution envisaged by EAM, which hitherto, it seems, the Greek Communist Party (KKE) seems to have controlled. Britain, on the other hand, through its BLOs and their control of weapons and gold (as Nicholas Hammond constantly emphasizes in his memoir), pressed ELAS to accelerate harassment of the Germans and interruption of communications and transport. But, in concert with Cairo, the BLOs were to maintain control and seemingly gener-

ate the schedule of operations.[26] ELAS was unwilling, however, to support every mission due to the German principle of savage reprisal.
ELAS was also fighting an off and on civil war with EDES, whose
leader Napoleon Zervas the British supported, and at the same time
was engaged in a no-quarter war with collaborators in Macedonia (see
Chapter 2).

The political situation in Greece was subject to forces far beyond its
borders. Britain was committed to restoring the king of Greece to his
throne. Churchill, for his part, was fascinated with the Balkan option
which, he hoped, would redeem the failed Gallipoli campaign of World
War I.[27] All Greeks, of course, were willing to die in order to redeem
the honor of Greece sullied by the occupation of the Italians, the
Germans, and the Bulgarians.[28] As an occupied country whose government served at Hitler's pleasure and which had been frequently
changed, the official Greek position was to pursue a war against the
Communists. The United States, on the other hand and for its own
political and strategic reasons, saw the path to the end of the war via
Italy and not Greece.[29]

Even so the Americans had a vested interest in Greece that began
with 'Wild Bill' Donovan's OSS plans for the country. We have seen
how these were developed initially by Ulius Amoss and then became a
regular venture paralleling, but subordinate to, the British show in
Greece (Chapter 3). Nonetheless the Americans through the
Evvoia–Çesme caique ferry service pursued their own plans to harass
the German retreat from Greece. The OSS files contain a series of
reports from local Greek Orthodox priests in the United States listing
military age American Greeks and their skills. From this pool a mostly
American-Greek battalion was recruited and from these, 159 enlisted
men and fifteen officers were sent into Greece on regular and long-
term missions from Bari and Çesme.[30]

A total of eight American Operational Groups were sent into
Greece from 23 April to 20 November 1944, which were active in
Epirus, Roumeli (southwest of Lamia), Thessaly (east of Ellason),
Macedonia (Drama), Paikon, Pierias (Olympus—Katarini), Macedonia
(Vermion), and Peloponnesus. The groups accounted for 76 operations
against the enemy with impressive statistics: they attacked 14 trains, 5
convoys, 15 bridges, and destroyed nearly 10 miles of railroad track;
killed 349, wounded 196, and captured 105. Only 13 Americans were
wounded. Many of these actions were supported by *andartes*, whether
explosives experts or infantry. It is clear from their reports that the support of the *andartes* was essential to their survival in the mountains if

not success in the field. Comparable figures for the British missions and their accomplishments in Operation Noah's Ark are not at present available. There were nearly 150 British missions active in Greece, and a number of them are mentioned in the American reports.

The caique ferry service from Çesme to Evvoia was exclusively American since the *andartes* on Evvoia did not trust the British, who were never able to establish a mission on the island. Moreover, the Americans in the field were all of Greek background, including many of the officers, and they did not display the arrogance characteristic of the BLOs. Even so, neither the British nor the Turks permitted the Americans to send in weapons or many supplies to ELAS. Their purpose was primarily to gain intelligence on the German battle order, print and distribute propaganda, lower German morale and instigate general mayhem through disinformation and sabotage, and work through the local *andartes*. The final reports on the American Mission (misnomered the Allied Mission, allowing the British to take the credit) testifies to the success of operation 'Smashem', conceived like Operation Noah's Ark to disrupt communications and harass the German retreat from Greece. Similar missions stretched through the Balkans into southern Austria; however, only those supported by Tito's partisans or Mihailovich's Chetniks were successful.[31] The reports allow us a running chronology of the actions against the Germans that parallel many of the actions recorded by General Sarafis in his official memoir and recalled by many of the *andartes* in their collective memories. A systematic comparison of Sarafis's missions with those of the Americans and the British will one day allow historians to clarify the specific roles of the Greek resistance (with its multinational cadre of volunteers – including Italian, Austrian, and German defectors, liberated Russian POWs, Bulgarian communists, fighting Balkan refugees, etc.) alongside the Allied war effort. This effort, however, should not detract from the war waged by the *andartiko* against the Italian, the German, and the Bulgarian occupiers and their collaborators.

The organizing of ELAS into a regular army under General Sarafis at last makes it possible occasionally to categorize the memoirs of Jewish *andartes* according to units and areas, and to chronicle the missions they recall or were involved in. Most of the survivors, whose memoirs were collected by Yad Vashem after their emigration to Israel or by Michael Matsas in his *Illusion of Safety*, were active in Boeotia (many from Athens), Thessaly (many from Volos, Larissa, and Trikala), and Macedonia (many from Salonika). Many of these *andartes* participated in the British operation called 'Animals' (summer 1943), which was promoted to fool Hitler into thinking that the proposed invasion of Sicily was actually aimed at an invasion of Greece. Even more so in Noah's Ark (summer 1944). The game was afoot, as Sherlock Holmes was wont to say, but the players were Greek *andartes*, and the many victims of German retaliation the mountain villagers and lowland hostages.

The plethora of German documents that record their punishing response to *andarte* attacks tends to obscure the futility of the effort.[32] 'Animals' successfully fooled the Germans and some 300,000 troops remained in Greece during the invasion of Italy. The 999 Strafbattalions and the SS brigades responded like automatons to guerrilla attacks. The principle was to exact vengeance according to Wehrmacht orders (100 hostages shot for each German killed and 10 for each wounded), although in Greece it was observed somewhat in the breech in the last year of the war. The trains that were derailed and the officers, including generals, killed or wounded during the process of German troop movements and evacuation, only aroused the *furor Teutonicus*.[33] Villages within reach of punishment reprisals were destroyed; women and aged men and children were butchered or burned in sealed churches. In one such raid in Acarnania a Jewish family invited by friends to a village wedding in Komona came to be numbered among the 300 victims of a reprisal.[34] By the war's end thousands of houses throughout Greece were listed as destroyed and nearly half a million Greeks were listed as wartime victims.[35] It was a brutal and ugly war in Greece, perhaps more so in Yugoslavia.

NOTES

1. Yad Vashem recently honored one of these recruiters, Alexandros Kallodopoulos, as a Righteous Gentile for his wartime rescue work.
2. Stephanos Sarafis, *ELAS. Greek Resistance Army* (London, 1980), p. 167 identifies the 50th Katerini Regiment: its *kapetanios* (military commander) Lt. Kikitsas and EAM *politikos* Markos Vafiades. The latter had recruited Joseph Matsas and other young Jews of Salonika. After August 1943, Col. Kalambakis became military commander.
3. Yosef Ben, *Yehudei yavan bashoah uvahitnagdut 1941–1944* (Greek Jewry in the Holocaust and Resistance) (Tel Aviv, 1985), pp. 130–2 contains a partial summary of YVS 03/2149/145.
4. Ben, *Greek Jewry*, p. 139.
5. The Kavalla–Salonika sequence of his memoir is in Michael Matsas, *Illusion of Safety* (New York, 1997), pp. 167 ff.
6. John O. Iatrides (ed.), *Greece in the 1940s. A Bibliographic Companion* (Hanover, NH and London, 1981), p. 86 #03/2990 and Ben, *Greek Jewry*, pp. 139–42 (#03-2651). (Yad Vashem renumbered its memoirs between the time I saw them in 1978 and Ben's research during the 1980s; hence the different numbers.) After their initial stay in a mountain village, the family returned to Larissa and then went back to the mountains after the Germans took over. They (his father, his wife, and her brother) were captured along with the men of the village and sent to Pavlos Melos in Salonika whence all, save Albert who had a false ID, were sent to a concentration camp in Germany.

7. Cf. Matsas, *Illusion of Safety*,p. 302. He was condemned to death after the war but escaped to Palestine where he became the director of Tnuva, the main cooperative for village produce under the aegis of the Histadruth. On the role of ETA, see Sarafis, *ELAS*, p. 265.

8. Compare the memoir of Matsas, *Illusion of Safety.*

9. Ben, *Greek Jewry*, pp. 137 f.

10. Ibid. p. 136. Gattegno was first interviewed by Miriam Novitch in 1959.

11. Slavophones in Macedonia organized and armed by the Germans. For the role of Lt. Anton Kaltchev and the complexities of Italian–Bulgarian–German policies in this area, see John S. Koliopoulos, *Plundered Loyalties. World War II and the Civil War in Greece West Macedonia* (New York, 1999), pp. 64–5 and *passim*. The two memoirs of Nicholas Hammond are essential: *The Allied Military Mission and the Resistance in West Macedonia* (Thessaloniki Institute for Balkan Studies, 1993), and *Venture into Greece with the Guerillas 1943–1944* (London, 1983).

12. It was decided on August 1, 1943 to establish the school, and each Headquarters and general command (later designated divisions and regiments) was to supply 30 *andartes*. The class of 136 graduated after a month; the second class began on October 1 with 300 cadets. Cf. Sarafis, *ELAS*, pp. 154 and 176. Each graduate became a platoon leader with the rank of second lieutenant.

13. Daisy Carasso (YVS 03/4542) gives a date of July 23, 1944, a date supported by Joseph Matsas, his *synagonistes*, who records in *Illusion of Safety*, p. 65, his other exploits; Sarafis, *ELAS*, records two incidents at Muharrem Hani (15 kilometers from Edessa in Macedonia) on 28 July (5 ELAS dead) and 6 August (2 ELAS dead). Sarafis records 24 German dead, but local Greek sources have published a figure of 250 (for the latter, cf. Yitzhak Mosheh's memoir in YVS 03/4542, and Ch. 2). His sister recorded that Greek students working at the Pavlos Melas prison gave him his father's watch and told him his last words.

14. Matsas, *Illusion of Safety*, p. 66.

15. Matsas dates this to July 2, 1944; cf. Sarafis, *ELAS*, p. 447 (correct date accordingly) for details.

16. Albert Cohen, Raphael Maltas, Leon Meir, Shlomo Matsil, Mosheh Cohen, and Aris Kazes ('Kolokotrone').

17. See H. Papanikolis, *I Maxi stis Karoutes 5.8.44* (Athens, 1983), non vidi.

18. Memoir in author's possession. This had to be in late September/early October since the Germans were destroying the railway to hinder the anticipated British pursuit. An American group under the command of Lt. Pappas, along with a group of *andarte* demolition men set out on October 6 to attack the nemesis called the Panzer-Zug, a powerful armored train that carried patrols out each dusk. Their attempt to ambush the train near Neo Monastirion was foiled when the Germans engaged them in a firefight. Two other demolition teams however succeeded in destroying a length of track. A week later their mission had changed to attacking the rear guard and preventing the Germans from destroying communications and roads to protect their retreat. Lt. Pappas was to provide security on the flank while the main *andarte* body attacked the train and a road convoy. Near the town of Kournaritsi they watched as the Germans blew up three railroad bridges and destroyed the track and telegraph lines. Just prior to the explosion two B-24 bombers had dropped a load on the area where two bridges were located. The *andartes* successfully attacked the convoy and inflicted considerable casualties on the enemy. NARA 226/99/45/5-Ops.

19. Joseph Matsas, Yoseh Ben, and the author have published partial lists of *andartes*; new material has been collected by Michael Matsas (See Appendix II). The testimonies at Yad Vashem have yet to be systematically exploited on this subject.

20. *ELAS*, p. 443; Steyers are Austrian submachine guns.

21. Matsas, *Illusion of Safety*, p. 65. The discrepancy in casualty figures may be due to the decision to take no German prisoners, and those captured were shot.

22. See Stavros B. Thomadakis, 'Black Markets, Inflation, and Force in the Economy of Occupied Greece', in Iatrides, *Greece in the 1940s*, pp. 61-80.

23. It is interesting that we do not find discussion of this point in the plethora of debriefings of refugees from Greece. We do read about inflation and prices, but not about such an organization.

24. Yad Vashem testimony #03-2630; partial summary in Ben, *Greek Jewry*, pp. 133–6; and summarized as 03/2989 in Iatrides, *Greece in the 1940s*, II, pp. 85–6.

25. How much the more so during the war. A comment on the reports of Brig. Myers, Cols Woodhouse and Stevens, Lt. Cols Hammond and McMullen, and Capt. Lake (Kew HS5/635

D/H 109) notes: 'It is to be noticed that most of these officers, with the notable exception of Brigadier Myers, found themselves owing to the policy which they were instructed to pursue vis-à-vis EAM/ELAS more or less in opposition to that organisation and this has in some cases considerably colored their views. This has been particularly noticeable in the Peloponnesus. It is, I think, of some importance that this bias should be taken into account.'

26. The Bashibazook exploit of Patrick L. Fermor and Stanley Moss to kidnap General Kreipe, the about-to-be-relieved German commander of Crete, resulted in the execution of a number of Cretan hostages including several Jews. The latter of course were *sub poine mortis* in any event. See Stanley W. Moss, *Ill-Met by Moonlight* (New York, 1950). Kreipe expressed relief at his capture since it meant the end of the war for him. The report of the OSS Royce mission that preceded their exploit has now been declassified (NARA 210/200/03). A hitherto unknown source may be noted here for the historical record. Ze'ev Haklai, *Im shevuyim rusim* (With Russian POWs) (Tel Aviv, 1945/6) records his interview with a Russian Jew, a POW who escaped to the *andartes* on Crete after a tour of the Reich as a slave worker). The latter (known as Michaelo on Crete) claimed to have led a group of Soviet POWs with the Cretan Resistance under the general leadership of Major Alex (pp. 61 ff.); some of these Russians participated in the exploit of the general's capture (p. 63).

27. Jan Smuts continuously emphasized to Churchill and Roosevelt the importance of Africa and the Middle East. With the former he had much in common in this position; not so with the latter. Churchill and Stalin would soon acknowledge in a formal agreement their division of the Balkans which both were to honor to the detriment of their erstwhile protégés in Greece (ELAS) and Yugoslavia (Mihailovich).

28. One should note here the parallel to the situation in Yugoslavia where the peasants who supported Tito asked for no quarter and gave none. On the other hand, Mihailovich's supporters had a tendency to passive and/or active collaboration with the occupiers by those who preferred to survive the war rather than defeat the Axis occupiers. Zervas's actions seem to fall into the latter catagory. Both male and female *andartes*, on the other hand, independently told me that war is war and civilians just might suffer the consequences (see above chapter 3). See now Franklin Lindsay, *Beacons in the Night. With the OSS and Tito's Partisans in Wartime Yugoslavia* (Stanford, 1993).

29. It is not improbable that the Italian option was as much a function of opportunity – Algeria to Tunisia to Sicily to Rome – as it was a function of domestic American politics, which had a larger Italian and Catholic population. The highly decorated Nisei brigade, for example, constituted from American-born Japanese, was willing to suffer incredible casualties to prove their loyalty on any European front. Even so, the US did recruit a small American Greek unit which served successfully in Greece during summer 1944; unfortunately the latter's story has not yet been told. The British perspective, which (traditionally) saw the US attitude as an opposition to British influence in the Balkans was first articulated in Chester Wilmot, *The Struggle for Europe* (London, 1952).

30. This was the 2671st Special Reconnaissance Battalion, Special (Provisional) with 107 officers and 676 enlisted men.

31. One into Austria and another in Slovakia were tragic failures.

32. Cf. John Hondros, *Occupation and Resistance: The Greek Agony, 1941–1944* (New York, 1983) and Mark Mazower, *Inside Hitler's Greece. The Experience of Occupation, 1941–1944* (New Haven and London, 1993), *passim*.

33. Perhaps one of Germany's more ironic wartime legacies is the German military cemetery on the road to Marathon where some 10,000 Wehrmacht and SS casualties lie buried in mass graves, each under the sign of a cross.

34. Cf. Mark Mazower, 'Military Violence and National Socialist Values,' *Past and Present* 134 (1992), pp. 129–58.

35. Cf. *Pinakes Katastrophon Oikodomon tes Hellados* (Lists of Greek Destroyed Homes). The State Department files from Cairo in NARA contain detailed lists of destroyed villages and war crimes.

Polis Politics: EAM in Motion

Jews were also active in various ways in the urban resistance that comprised much of the Greek population. Sometime haphazardly, as Sam Nahmias and an Orthodox friend who at the age of 12 or 13 painted slogans on the walls in Athens recalled. The boys retired to more less noticeable pastimes after learning that people were shot for such activities.[1] Others were more organized, for example Alhi Refael of Athens who in response to EPON recruiters volunteered (at age 14) to paint such slogans as 'Death to the Conqueror'. Armed adults protected the young boys and girls. Occasionally, when the paint ran out, the children attempted to complete the words with their own blood. Some fell in the process...[2]

In addition to propaganda there was also sabotage. Isaac (Zak) Kostis, a student of law who had literary aspirations, was part of a clandestine group that dynamited enemy ships in Piraeus and elsewhere.[3] These included a German B103 troop carrier in Keratsini, the *Cyclops* in Piraeus harbor, the *Ardenas*, K273 cargo vessels and the *Orion*, and the tugboat *Taxiarhis*. After the war he was decorated for his exploits.

Even before the conquest of Greece, Jews contributed to the fight against the Germans. Aside from those who fought in the mountains against the Italians or protected the withdrawal of the British in their disastrous retreat to Corinth, Kalamata, and then Crete for the final battle that renewed for that island the slogan 'Freedom or Death,' there were others in the rear. For instance, Dr Ernst Müller, a German Jewish gynecologist, who was the only refugee doctor to obtain a Greek medical license (under the name of Myller) and become a Greek citizen. He opened a hospital for women in Athens, which the Nazis paradoxically recommended as the German hospital in Greece. That advertisement, his linguistic and medical skills, and his contacts among the Athens elite contributed to its success. Among his friends and supporters was Dr Logothetopoulos, Head of Gynecology at the University of Athens, who had also studied in Germany.

Müller's wife Liselotte listed his two contributions to the Allied war effort, which the British rewarded by rescuing him on the last Allied boat, the *Warsowa*, that left Athens on April 27, 1941.[4] The first was his invention of an antidote to the German device that successfully countered the British ability to detect sea mines. The second came as a result of a visit to the hospital from a Lufthansa pilot who bragged to him about an imminent airborne invasion of Crete by glider. Immediately, Müller crossed the street and informed the British ambassador whom he knew well. Liselotte made her own important contributions. First was her public protest at the exclusion of Jews from EON, Metaxas's national youth organization. The ban, she averred, was lifted after a few weeks and the ministers responsible for it were removed. She also assisted Renato Mordo, Director of the Prague Opera, to return to Greece and develop major opera in Athens. And after resettling in the United States she was active in Greek war relief. The anecdotal nature of her memoir is a good indication how policy was effected in Greece during the inter-war years.

After the occupation of Salonika by the Germans, officers were quartered in middle- and upper-class homes (The Gestapo of course confiscated those mansions that interested them). Many of these officers found themselves in Jewish homes, occasionally among Jews who spoke German. While relations were generally friendly, given the courtesy of old-line Austrian officers, military information slipped out regularly and was reported to resistance circles who passed it on to Cairo. A number of Jewish memoirs report on such activity, which is paralleled by memoirs from similar situations in Athens.

While the above exploits were part of a mass response to resistance from men, women, and children throughout Greece, a number of individuals acted in a variety of ways that show urban Jews using what skills they had to lead their communities during the occupation. Barukh Shibi and Sam Modiano were journalists from Salonika who spent the war years in Athens. Also in Athens was Asher Moissis, a prominant Salonikan lawyer who was the last elected president of the Jewish community of Salonika (removed from office by Metaxas in 1936), and an active Zionist.[5]

In 1927 Shibi had established the Zionist club 'Ahduth' which soon had branches in the various Jewish neighborhoods and attracted the lower classes. Following the visit of A. Reiss in 1935, a branch of the World Union of Poalei Zion was formed that soon absorbed 'Ahduth' and another Zionist club 'Max Nordau' and emerged as a socialist base within the community in support of the Jewish settlement of Palestine. On the eve of the German invasion Shibi, aware that he was on the Gestapo's wanted list, fled Salonika with the retreating British. He reached Crete along with Greek parliamentary deputies Mentesh Besantsi[6] and Jacques Ventura (both were subsequently captured);[7] but, unable to embark to Egypt, Shibi returned to Athens. Soon he began working with the newly formed EAM, and became one of the leaders for Sector 3A.[8] He was influential in having prominent Greeks stop the publication of an anti-Semitic economic weekly. One of his early projects (during 1942-3) was to translate the works of Professors Zakythinos and Keramopoulos, which were to be used after the war as a reply to the Bulgarian claims for Macedonia and Thrace.[9] Shibi also reported to a semi-underground committee on pro-German activities among Greek intellectuals; later he was commissioned to write reports on such activities. His EAM unit (which included Jews and Greeks)[10] was soon printing an underground newspaper and pamphlets. Some material was aimed specifically at the Jewish problem in Salonika, while warnings were printed advising the Athenian Jews not to report to the German-controlled synagogue in Athens.[11] Shibi would be instrumental, according to his memoir, in the abduction/escape of Rabbi Barzilai from Athens (see below).

After General Jürgen Stroop, who had presided over the destruction of the Warsaw ghetto, established his presence in Athens, the lawyers' union assisted Shibi to escape to the Peloponnesus where he joined a resistance unit. In February 1944 he tried to convince Louvaris to leave the government and join the resistance. After all, Shibi argued, he was a known friend of the Jews and a patriot. Louvaris responded that he could not leave the church without a protector in the government. Such was one problem for those who had to serve in a collaborationist government. Shibi returned to Arcadia in the Peloponnesus where he administered the resistance newspapers throughout the region and functioned as one of the three leaders in the area. During Passover 1944, the Germans began a sweep against the *andartiko* and trapped their units near Gortini. The Greeks called up the reserves and inflicted a major defeat on a 700-strong unit of regulars at the Battle of Glogoba; the other units retreated.[12]

Sam Modiano, who had Italian citizenship, was active with a number of organizations in Salonika, some within the Italian Consulate, others independent Greek organizations consisting of army officers, and with a special unit of MO5.[13] The latter, according to Modiano, had parachuted a South African named George Bauer, a personal friend of Fieldmarshal Ian Smuts, to organize Greek resistance in Macedonia. Modiano's cousin by marriage, a full colonel in the Greek army, sent Bauer, via a trusted Greek named Argyropoulos, to Modiano, who in turn passed him on to Fidel Kondopolis, the husband of one of Modiano's nieces.[14] Modiano was also able, through his son, who had been drafted into the Jewish police unit organized by the Jewish collaborator Hasson, to get some food to Jacques Ventura, under arrest in Baron Hirsch, on the night before he was deported to Auschwitz.[15]

Modiano's memoir is interesting since he claims not to have belonged to any specific organization but rather acted on his own through an extensive network of friends and relatives. In other words, his initiative allowed him to be a liaison between different organizations and yet remain sufficiently autonomous to pursue his own goals. Modiano had been an important figure in inter-war Greek politics, especially in Salonika, as a 'personal friend' of Venizelos, and as a liaison with Jewish business leaders through his journalistic contacts. Modiano also claims that the Italian consulate in Salonika was collaborating with the British, who had their own agent in the consulate under the alias of Alfred Rosenberg(!).[16] The Italians, in any event, certified that Modiano was both Italian born and an Italian military officer. They gave him papers identifying him as head of a consulate department for the Jews of Italian origin that allowed him and his people to issue false papers for 350 Jewish families, enabling them to get on the last Italian military train that left Salonika. With a wink in his eye, he proudly claimed that the train was supplied personally by Mussolini whom he knew from the latter's days as a journalist.[17] Later in Athens (presumably after October 1944) the British gave him papers as a war correspondent with the rank of brevet captain in the British army, under which façade he was able to help organize the Hagganah mission which accompanied the British forces in 1944.[18]

Asher Moissis was a lawyer for the Jewish community in Athens. He was also a personal friend and sometime partner of the Salonika-based Yomtov Yacoel who served as the lawyer for the Jewish community.[19] Moissis preserved and later published Yacoel's invaluable occupation memoir which Yacoel entrusted to him before being deported to Auschwitz. Moissis later authenticated the testimony as evidence in the Eichmann trial.[20]

As a successful lawyer, Moissis had many contacts among Greek politicians and intellectuals. He shows in his memoir how the support of the Greek government, church, professional organizations, and university was orchestrated during the occupation to protest against the deportation of the Salonika Jews.[21] Indeed, notwithstanding the desire of many Greeks to assist Jews who were after all fellow Greeks, it appears that it was necessary for Jews themselves to encourage their potential and willing allies into activities which might help them to save. This point is lacking in both general and Jewish literature on the war.

It appears that Jews with access to Christians on a comparable professional level approached them to make public statements in behalf of the Jews. General Tsolakoglou's words reflect as much the Jewish perception of the situation as his own. In April 1942, he came to Salonika and promised: 'Nothing will happen to you, you are Greeks, we are all brothers and sisters, you are the children of our Beloved (Patrida) Country, many of you died and were wounded fighting the enemy.'[22] Professor Logothetopoulos as well as Ioannis Rhalles voiced the same sentiments when each served in turn as puppet leader of occupied Greece. Asher Moissis sheds light on these interventions in his postwar memoir, which provides valuable insight into the times:[23]

> On March 13, 1943, Visliceny(!) and Brunner called Coretz(!) and told him that two days later the dispatch of Jews would be transported to Baron Hirsch ... Lawyer Yomtov Jacquel [i.e., Yacoel] lawyer of the Jewish community telephoned me to Athens, notified me as to what was happening for the first deportation of the Baron Hirsch. What steps did we take? We went to Archbishop Damaskinos – Damaskinos was in bed, but he saw me and said he would talk to Altenburg in Athens (Altenburg was the Nazi Commissioner of Greece). Altenburg told him that he could do nothing because the order came from Berlin. The prime minister then was Logothetopoulos who was a Germanophile (now in prison). All the leaders of the political parties wrote a petition to Logothetopoulos asking him to intervene and to ask of the Germans not to persecute the Jews because Jews were Greek citizens and in Greece there was no discrimination between Jews and Greeks. Logothetopoulos went to Altenburg and he told him what he had told Damaskinos. He made a note of protestation to Altenburg which Altenburg said he would send to Berlin. On the fifteenth or sixteenth of March, Asher Moissis went to Logothetopoulos together with Rabbi Barzilai and Albert Amarillio and we took with us Tsaldaris[24] who was my friend, as well as the friend of Logothetopoulos. I spoke very forcefully to Logothetopoulos and he said, 'What can I do, I am very upset about it.'[25] Then I told him, 'If it is for the Jews to die, because they are going to their death, then they have the right to ask of the Greek government to die inside Greece, and not to go out of Greece to unknown places.' I yelled so loud that all the other

personel gathered around so that Logothetopoulos fell into his chair.[26] The result of that was for me to write a note of protestation. The dispatching of the Jews had begun. I saw Logothetopoulos, and Tsaldaris was with me, twice again.[27] Tsaldaris helped us very much. Then we decided to ask Logothetopoulos to resign with the whole government. 32 other organizations, professional, labor and scientific academy asked for his resignation, headed by Damaskinos and the church. Through Tsaldaris, Logothetopoulos sent me that he would like to resign, but the Jewish problem was the 'weak point of Hitler' and he didn't want to leave the impression with the Germans that he was resigning because of the Jews. After fifteen days, the Germans put Logothetopoulos out of office and they appointed Rallis, prime minister. As soon as Rallis took the oath of office, after great pressure on our parts and on the part of the political leaders, especially on the part of Kavandaris,[28] leader of the Liberal Progressive Party, he went to Salonika to take up the matter of the Jewish persecution. But he could do nothing. The Nazis would not listen to him. He remained there only one night. The Nazis would not listen to him.

Archbishop Damaskinos was also approached by Jews and these leaders to make a statement.[29] In February 1943, Rabbi Koretz and several Jewish lawyers independently approached the Archbishop of Macedonia, Metropolitan Gennadios, to intervene with the Germans. On the eve of Rhallis's flying visit to Salonika, Koretz prevailed on Archbishop Gennadios to arrange a meeting with the prime minister and later, in a tear-filled interview, saw Rhallis. Koretz's demeanor so angered the Nazis that they arrested him and interned him and his family in Baron Hirsch.[30] What is important here is not that these meetings and public statements were ineffective with the Germans, but that they were heard ultimately by the Greek people. The statements were as effective in retrospect, if not more so from the Archbishop to his clergy, as the statements broadcast over the BBC to occupied Greece.[31]

The swelling of the Athenian Jewish population with refugees from the Bulgarian and German zones brought new wealth and influence to the community. Perhaps as many as 5,000 Jews found their way to the capital, and, since these were among the wealthy of Salonika, it was to them that Yomtov Yacoel turned when money was needed to ransom the Jews in the forced labor that had been imposed in mid-July 1942.

At the same time a continual stream of wealthy Jews made their escape to Cairo. Ambassador MacVeagh sent a series of reports to President Roosevelt in 1943 and 1944 outlining the situation of the Jews in Greece through summaries of talks given by these refugees to Jews and Greeks in Cairo. It is from them that we learn that the Italians and the Greek police protected the Jews from attacks by pro-German groups in Athens and from the efforts of the Gestapo to enforce their persecutions on Athenian Jewry.

Most of the pro-German groups, including ESPO, EEE, and other Fascist/Nazi gangs, bribed and extorted money from Jewish businessmen. In December 1942 agents of ESPO sacked the Jewish community offices in Athens and destroyed or carried off its records. The community council disbanded and an unofficial committee was formed to watch over community concerns. Shortly thereafter Kostas Perrikos, an anti-Nazi, bombed ESPO headquarters, and a number of Jewish leaders were imprisoned in retaliation. The Italian authorities were contacted, and they were subsequently released. The loss of the community rosters was to benefit the Athenian Jews during September 1943 when the Gestapo demanded them from Rabbi Barzilai. Higher SS and Police Leader General Jürgen Stroop was now in Athens after the Italian surrender, along with Walter Blume as commander of the SiPo/SD, to facilitate the deportation of the Athenian Jews. Rabbi Barzilai was summoned to Gestapo headquarters and ordered to hand over the community registers. According to Barzilai's postwar account, he took this opportunity to argue that ESPO had destroyed them the previous year.[32] In his memoir, he avers that he heard the Gestapo discussing the deportations, a discussion he understood since he had studied in Jerusalem and learned some German there. When he was released with the order to produce new lists, he went home and passed the message that Jews should flee to the mountains ('The old man is sick and needs to go the mountains to recuperate.'). Over the weekend of September 23, 1943 he claims that he escaped with the aid of Archbishop Damaskinos. The resistance role is not mentioned.

Modiano and Shibi provide further background to this episode that alters somewhat the atmosphere of the rabbi's story, which has entered into Jewish historiography as a counterpoint to the failure of Rabbi Koretz to do something similar in Salonika.[33]

Shibi avers that he kidnapped the rabbi with some colleagues from EAM. This was in anticipation of the arrival of General Stroop. Schibi informed Joseph Nehama, a member of the Community Council, who agreed to the project, and he also asked permission from the Central

Committee of EAM. Shibi and the Athenian journalist Kostas Vidalis worked out the details. Then Shibi contacted Professor Nikos Louvaris, the Minister for Religious Affairs, to intervene with Archbishop Damaskinos, who immediately offered his hospitality to the rabbi. Accordingly Ilias Kefalides, a lawyer from Salonika, and Salomon Sasson were designated to hide him in the Dexameni Quarter of Athens from where, disguised as a Greek merchant, he and his family were escorted by Kapetan Makkabaios to the forces of Lieutenant Demitrios Demitriou ('Nikephoros').[34]

Modiano, who was informed by his friend Paul Noah[35] that the Rosenberg Kommando had come from Salonika to capture Rabbi Barzilai, went to EAM. The organization then contacted Kostas Vidalis, editor of the communist *Eleftheri Ellada* and an executive member of the Communist Party.[36] Vidalis at this point, and unbeknownst to Modiano, went to Shibi and made final arrangements. Two armed men, one of them Isidore Noah, went to the rabbi's house and told him to prepare to leave. According to Mary Noah, Isidore's wife, they were prepared to use their weapons on the rabbi.[37] As Shibi told me in 1972, 'One more rabbi or less would not be missed; but it was important that he leave.' In a letter to Michael Matsas, Shibi ascribed this statement to Joseph Nehama. The rabbi was driven out of the city, apparently in the archbishop's car, and transferred to a truck (EAM used postal trucks as a cover) which brought him to the hills. Kapetan 'Makkabaios' then escorted him mounted on a donkey to the BLO Chris Woodhouse. Barzilai's statements on behalf of EAM–ELAS and calls for aid to the Resistance were widely reported resulting, it seems, in an OSS investigation as to whether the rabbi was indeed a Communist.[38]

It emerges from a conflation of these separate stories that a) the Gestapo wanted Barzilai to cooperate; b) the Jews in the resistance did not want to give him the opportunity; c) Jews worked with EAM leaders and government officials to secure his escape; d) Jews were privy to considerable secret information through their contacts that they were able to exploit with a little initiative. The reaction is more important than the details, however. The disappearance of the rabbi shocked the community into an awareness of the danger that they faced such that they took heed of resistance warnings to stay away from the synagogue. Many followed the rabbi's lead, as they understood his disappearance, and went to the mountains. The plan actively pursued by the Salonikan Jews in the resistance was successful in avoiding the possible repeat of the loss of nerve coupled with naivete that had already contributed to the destruction of their beloved community.[39]

NOTES

1. Interview with the author in 1989. There was no mention of an organizational structure behind this act and its spontaneity is paralleled by numerous other recollections in the literature.
2. Testimony of Alhi Refael in *Lo Nishkach*, 11 (1996), p. 13 (in Hebrew).
3. Kostis published a literary version of his exploits. See Isaac Kostis ... *Ptyches*.... (Athens, 1968). See also Michael Matsas, *Illusion of Safety* (New York, 1997), p. 295; Yosef Ben, *Greek Jewry in the Holocaust and the Resistance 1941–1944* (Tel Aviv, 1985), p. 129.
   The group may have been connected with the Apollo network that ultimately received a DSO (see Kew HS5/737).
4. Liselotte Khan *The Memoirs of Liselotte Kahn* (New York, 1996), pp. 58, 68 ff. and *passim*. Further research in the British Archives may illuminate her memoir. As for the invasion, Churchill was already aware of it through the Enigma sources deciphered at Bletchley Park. The Greek portion of the memoir covers the period from 1934 to 1941.
5. His successor was Rafael Halevi. The Germans subsequently appointed Saby Saltiel, an accountant. In December 1942 Rabbi Koretz was installed as president of the community despite his reluctance and the protests of the community leaders. For his literary career see my 'The Contribution of Asher Raphael Moisses,' *Studies in Bibliography and Booklore* 12(1979), pp. 25–7.
6. He was editor of 'Le Progrès' in Salonika, and according to Henry Levy, his house was turned into a Gestapo jail.
7. He was the first Jewish Communist to serve in the Greek Parliament and was later captured in Crete by Greek newsmen who were undercover police agents. The Germans interned him in the ghetto in the Baron Hirsch Quarter whence he was deported to Auschwitz.
8. The region bounded by St Constantin Street, Piraeus Street, and Iera Odos Streets; it also included the quarters of Botanikos and St George.
9. A council of nine professors presided over by Nikos Louvaris (which met in the building where General Darkos lived on Odos Nikis) commissioned these works on the recommendation of the university.
10. Greek Jews are of course Greeks. Convention and convenience, however, has established a style of denoting a distinction between Greek Jews and Greek Christians and Greek Communists (Jews were to be found among all three categories!). My usage, while uncomfortable to me and to most Greek Jews, maintains the convention with the caveat that its usage in no way connotes a difference in nationality or loyalty between Jewish and non-Jewish Greeks. The problem is that the phrase 'Jews and Greeks' used by Paul in his letters actually refers to monotheists and polytheists in the context. Once Greeks became Christians the phrase changed its meaning to support exclusion of the Jews from Christian society. Hence the reader must be aware of the context of the use of this ambivalent phrase. For example, Archbishop Damaskinos used the phrase to call for support and protection of the Greek Jews.
11. The General Secretary of EAM (identified only as Hatzi) agreed to a special edition of *Eleftheri Hellada* (edited by Kostas Vidalis who was also a friend of Sam Modiano) on the persecution of Salonika Jewry, but, according to Shibi, the project was canceled due to the fears of prominent Athenian Jews to make themselves obvious in case of reprisal. Cf. his memoir in Miriam Novitch, *Passage des barbares*. In the Hebrew version of his memoir, *Greek Jewry in the Holocaust. Memoirs* (Tel Aviv, 1988), p. 356, the paper is identified as *Meiioda Elephteri*. One of these warnings was recently discovered as insulation in an electric box in Athens and is located now in the Jewish Museum of Greece.
12. In December 1944 he returned to Athens, was arrested by the British, and interned in Egypt where he was elected to represent the 2,000 Greek prisoners there. After liberation he returned to organize the Jewish refugees in Salonika prior to becoming head of the Jewish community.
13. So Modiano identified the organization; his memory may have been faulty on this point. See Daniel Carpi, *Italian Diplomatic Documents on the History of the Holocaust in Greece 1941–1943)*(Tel Aviv University, 1999), *passim*.
14. The colonel in the Greek army was running an organization for a former air minister of the Greek government whose purpose was to rescue British officers and men trapped in Greece. Smuts, according to his son in *Jan Christian Smuts* ([London, 1952], pp. 414 f.) spent some time

in Cairo, and generally throughout the war looked after Greek affairs. Further research might clarify this episode. There is no mention of it in John S. Koliopoulos, *Plundered Loyalties. World War II and Civil War in Greece West Macedonia* (New York, 1999).

15. Ventura had been subeditor at Modiano's French language newspaper *L'Independent* before it was shut down by Metaxas in 1940. Modiano's memoir avers there were 100 Jews in the police unit; another source lists 200.

16. He could not recall whether it was MO4 or MO5. Actually Rosenberg's first name was Riccardo and he was with the Italian secret service. Cf. 'Excerpts from the Salonika Diary of Lucillo Merci (February–August 1943)' compiled by Joseph Rochlitz with introduction by Menahem Shelach, *Yad Vashem Studies*, Vol. XVII (Jerusalem, 1987). Steinberg's exhaustive research in the Italian sources produced no clue to his identity. See Jonathan Steinberg, *All or Nothing: The Axis and the Holocaust 1941–1943* (London and New York, 1990).

17. See documents on the organized flight of the Italian Jews to Athens in Daniel Carpi (ed.), *Italian Diplomatic Documents on the History of the Holocaust in Greece (1941–1943)*, s.v. Sam Modiano.

18. Karen McKay interviewed Modiano in July 1977, and there is a typescript in the Institute of Contemporary Jewry, Oral History Division at the Hebrew University of Jerusalem along with the original tapes (# C/1361-C/1366). I had several meetings with Modiano in 1972 and 1973. Modiano was interviewed in depth by Richard Capell in late 1944 (*Simiomata, A Greek Note Book 1944–1945*, (London, 1946). Capell provides better background to Modiano's escape and experiences in Athens than do the latter's later interviews. See Carpi, *Italian Diplomatic Documents*, s.v.

19. Both were from Trikkala.

20. State of Israel. Ministry of Justice, *The Trial of Adolf Eichmann. Record of the Proceedings in the District Court of Jerusalem*, II (repub. Jerusalem, 1992), pp. 847 f.; the Hebrew version translated by Moissis appeared in *Zikhron Saloniki* and elsewhere. Moissis has indicated that after Yacoel's escape to Athens he arranged for Yacoel to write his report. (Unfortunately he was arrested in mid-sentence, yet for some reason the manuscript was not confiscated.) Hence it is not a *diary* (as in the Hebrew and Greek editions, but rather it must be seen as a somewhat apologetic reflection upon events and personalities before the deportations. Yacoel was, after all, quite active in his capacity as lawyer for the community. It was he who drew up documents, interacted with officials, and apparently drew up the schedule of neighborhoods for deportation (the actual notes, in his hand, are extant, as related to me by Heinz Kounio). A full study of his role is a desideratum. The Hebrew version by Asher Moissis appeared in 1988. The English translation of his memoir, made from the Greek original (edited with extensive notes by Frangiski Abatzopoulou in 1993) is in *The Holocaust in Salonika. Eyewitness Accounts*, ed. Steven Bowman (New York, 2002).

21. Yad Vashem E/1187 is cited below. Moissis left several reports in French in his capacity as postwar head of the community.

22. Cited by Henry Levi, 'The Jews of Salonika and the Holocaust', Yale University, Sterling Memorial Library, Holocaust Testimonies.

23. Yad Vashem E/1187.

24. Constantine Tsaldaris, leader of the Populist Party, and active member of the prewar and postwar Greek governments.

25. It is interesting to note that Rhallis said almost the same thing to Edgar Thomashausen after the deportations of the Athenian Jews (interview with author in 1988).

26. In December 1994 I asked Daniel Bennahmias about this incident. He had worked for Moissis after the war and reported that such aggressive action was well within the bounds of his character. Liselotte Kahn's memoir indicates that Professor Logothetopoulos would have been unprepared to react to such an attack.

27. Moissis also 'asked Logothetopoulos to order Simonides [Governor of Macedonia] not to work with the Nazis for this purpose [the destruction of the Jewish cemetery]. Logothetopoulos told Moissis that he would send Simonides a telegram, and ask him for a report of the deportation of the Jews, but Simonides not only did not obey the orders but he did not send a report. He remained in office as governor until the liberation'. (YVS E/1187). On Simonides and his attitude toward the Jews, see now Andrew Apostolou, ' "The Exception of Salonika": Bystanders and Collaborators in Northern Greece,' *Holocaust and Genocide Studies*, 14, 2, (fall 2000), pp. 179 ff.

28. George Kafandaris was active in prewar and postwar Greek governments.

29. Actually, it was the Jewish wife of George Politis who proposed during an underground meeting of Greek intellectuals, professionals, and politicians that the Archbishop be approached. They all signed on behalf of their organizations in a protest that perhaps is unique for occupied Europe. See Matsas, *Illusion of Safety*, pp. 55 ff. for details, and for further on Mrs Politis see my *Agony of Greek Jewry during World War II* (forthcoming), Ch. 9.

30. According to Asher Moissis, 'Coretz was removed when he went to see Rallis because the Nazis saw that he was not the blind instrument for the Nazis and they appointed Albala' (YVS E/1187).

31. See my *Agony of Greek Jewry*, ch. 9 and above, Ch. 3.

32. Barouh Ouziel (ed.), *Guinzach Saloniki (Archives Saloniciennes)*, Fasc. A, (Tel Aviv, 1961), 90–2; repr. in *Greek Jewry in the Holocaust: Memoirs* (Tel Aviv, 1988), pp. 23–6. An English translation by the author is available in the Gennadeion Library.

33. Joseph Ben, 'Jewish Leadership in Greece during the Holocaust,' in *Patterns of Jewish Leadership in Nazi Europe 1933–1945* (Jerusalem), pp. 335–53.

34. See Ch. 3.

35. He had been ADC to Modiano in Salonika and, after coming to Athens, had befriended the chief of Italian intelligence. His memoir can be found at the Hebrew University of Jerusalem. Institute for Contemporary Jewry. Oral History Division, 25 (146).On the Noah brothers, see Ch. 1.

36. Vidalis told Modiano the story after the escape had been made. Cf. See note 18 on Karen McKay's 1977 interview..

37. Interview with the author in 1990.

38. Cf FO 371/43689, 236 ff. dated 21–2 July, 1944.

39. See Ch. 3 n. 19.

In Auschwitz: Joseph Varouh

The *andartiko* and the civil war were fought within the national borders of Greece. But Greeks fought and served in the wider theaters of the war and even forged legends in the concentration camps. It is not the theme of this book to follow the story of the Greek Brigades in Africa and Asia and to outline their contributions to the war effort. These men were part of the regular Greek army and navy that served under British control. The complexity of their vicissitudes is a combination of the ongoing stasis between the Right and the Left and British over-all policy toward the Left. British military discipline was more severe than British diplomacy and so had little patience for the finer points of Greek concepts of democracy. Hence these forces in which Greek Jews also served are not part of our story.

Nor are the thousands of Greek Christians, primarily from Crete, and others from the mainland who were sent to Mauthausen and its vicious subcamps Melk and Ebensee part of our tale. None of the Greeks sent there or to Theresienstadt or Dachau ever revolted against the prison regime that slowly destroyed them. Nor shall we dwell upon the tragedy of the 65,000 Greek Jews who were deported to Auschwitz and Treblinka where 90 percent were killed on arrival in gas chambers of varying efficiency. Among them were numerous veterans of the Albanian war including amputees who had had limbs removed because of frostbite caused by fighting in subzero temperatures, or because of the fighting itself. The latter's prosthetic limbs remain on display in the museum of the main camp of Auschwitz.[1] Rather we shall follow the heroic trail of those Greek Jews who overcame their slavery to fight against the Nazis in Warsaw and in Auschwitz.

The Warsaw story is relatively unknown. It began in September 1943 when Greek Jewish slaves were sent to the ruins of the Warsaw Ghetto to clean up and recycle the building materials that remained after the revolt in April 1943. Jews from other nationalities were later added to their numbers. Conditions were generally better than in the concentration camps: better food, a hospital, less sadistic guards, and opportunity to find hidden wealth that could be traded for more food.

But it was still dangerous. The work could be deadly as when individuals were sent atop the remaining wall of a building and ordered to rock it back and forth until it fell. And there was always the threat of disease. Yet the young Greeks were strong and many survived. In July 1944 the Nazis began to pull back and the ensuing death march witnessed thousands of slave workers on their way to Dachau (less than 300 Greeks survived the march). There remained in Warsaw about 500 prisoners, including some 78 Greek Jews.[2]

As the Nazis removed the main body of their slaves from Warsaw in the face of the Soviet advance, the Polish resistance within the city under the leadership of General Ber Komorovski stepped up preparations for a revolt that they anticipated would be supported by the Soviet army drawn up across the Vistula. At the beginning of August the revolt broke out. For months the Soviet army sat across the Vistula and watched the Nazis and the Poles kill each other. During the chaos a number of Greek Jews took the opportunity to escape from their captors and join the fighting. Their battle skills hard-won on the slopes of the Albanian mountains were a welcome addition to the handful of Polish veterans that led the revolt. After all, they knew how to drive tanks, to load cannon, to shoot rifles, to keep their head down and not panic, skills lacking among the Polish youth that joined the fight. Moreover they maintained that Greek elan of desperately brave fighting that had terrified the Italians and had impressed both the British who fought alongside them and the Germans against whom they held their ground so well.

A number of them survived to record the participation of Greek Jews in the second rebellion of Warsaw against the Nazis.
Albert Levi(#113135) and his brother Dario(#113134) were deported on April 3 from Salonika and after seven days arrived in Auschwitz; later they were sent in the second transport of Greeks to Warsaw. Alberto and Alberto Giladi escaped the work camp to join the partisans; Dario Levi and Leon El Porto later joined them and along with a lad identified only as Mois fought alongside several Polish Jews. The Greeks decided to break up into smaller units so that some might survive. One group even fought under a Greek flag that they fashioned. The Poles used some of them as shock troops to lead charges against German positions. The animosity toward Jews in general and to them in particular is recalled in the memoirs of those who survived, according to one account a mere 27.

Meanwhile in Auschwitz, in the subcamp called Birkenau that was the killing center for the deported Jews, plans were being made throughout the summer of 1944 for a revolt. The summer of 1944 was particularly intense. On the one hand, the Hungarian Jews were arriving by the hundreds of thousands; ultimately nearly half a million would be gassed and burned that summer. On the other hand, the resistance was well aware of the Soviet advance and anticipated an uprising to assist its liberation of the Auschwitz camp complex. There were three separate groups planning revolt. One was the main camp resistance represented by the Polish contingent that controlled much of the prisoner infrastructure. It was they who communicated with the outside world and sent information about the slaughter of the Jews and identified the perpetrators and picked targets for Allied bombers. The second was the Jewish underground that understandably was weak and dependent upon the Polish resistance leadership. The third was the Sonderkommando that consisted of the young strong men picked to service the gas chambers and the ovens. Only they would have the strength and the cohesiveness to initiate the fighting stage of the revolt.

The story of the XIth Sonderkommando is etched deeply in the historiography of Auschwitz even though the details are still somewhat confused. Three photographs, two often reproduced, of the horrific activities of the Sonderkommando have survived. These were taken in the summer of 1944 in a series of attempts to document and inform the world of the systematic slaughter occurring in Birkenau. According to survivors, a Greek Jew actually snapped the pictures.[3] The XIth Sonderkommando, morever, was the only one to revolt, despite the knowledge available to each group that worked in the crematoria that every previous Sonderkommando had been eliminated (with some individual exceptions) after approximately three or four months service. The question why only 1 out of 13 Sonderkommandos revolted necessitates a detailed analysis of the psychology and circumstances of each group, something that has yet to be done (if indeed it is even possible). The presence of Greeks in the XIth Sonderkommando may have been an important factor in making a revolt possible. Revolts have to be organized and preferably by those with military training: after all, revolts of the enslaved are usually against an organized and disciplined military. Already at a disadvantage, and only desperation would lead them to revolt, it is axiomatic that the slave revolts had to have the input of men who had undergone military training and at least a baptism of fire.[4] Many of the Jews who fought in Warsaw and those who fought in Auschwitz were veterans of the Greek campaign against the Italians fought in the snows of Albania. A detailed reading of the extant sources shows the presence of ex-officers and enlisted men in the 1944

Warsaw revolt and in the October revolt in Auschwitz (also Sobibor and Treblinka). That they were outnumbered and desperate does not detract from their heroism. As we noted earlier, all true heroes in Greek tradition are dead heroes.

The first incidents of Greek rebellion, albeit passive, came from one of the last Greek transports to Auschwitz. The influx of Hungarian Jews necessitated an increase in the numbers of the Sonderkommando and so 400 (or 435) Greeks were selected. Without any indoctrination, they were assigned to the crematorium, but when their assignment was explained to them they refused, even after being threatened with death. They were all killed, but their story was preserved by the Greek Jews and by others in the camp. Greek sources recall another 100 who also refused and were killed. The second incident was more active, although it was an individual case. Alberto Errara, a former officer in the Greek army, was part of a squad sent to empty the ashes from the crematoria in the Vistula. He attacked the guards and leaped into the river but was wounded during the attempted escape. Later he was captured and brought back to the camp and executed before the assembled prisoners according to standard policy.[5]

Errara's action, according to Leon Cohen who survived to write his memoir of the Sonderkommando and the revolt, impressed the Russian prisoners and convinced them to join in the revolt.[6] Meanwhile, plans for the revolt were sabotaged and delayed by informers and the question remains whether there would even have been a revolt. On the one hand, the Soviet advance had stopped outside Warsaw and outside of Lodz thus allowing the Poles and Germans to kill each other in the former and the Nazis to deport to Auschwitz some 68,000 Jews from the latter. Hence the Polish resistance in Auschwitz was cautious about initiating a revolt that might have led to the murder of all its inmates. The desperate Jewish resistance could do little without their support, although the Jewish girls from the Union Factory that produced munitions for Krupp succeeded in smuggling dynamite to the Sonderkommando. The general resistance, including perhaps the Allied POWs in the main camp, assisted with a few light weapons.[7] By the end of the summer the Hungarian flood had ceased and the pragmatic Nazis decided to reduce the size of the Sonderkommando.

According to reconstructions of the revolt, by the end of September 1944 there were 663 men in the Sonderkommando.[8] On September 24, 200 were selected, then tricked into a room in the Kanada area and gassed. Their bodies were secretly burned in crematorium 2 by the SS guards. The disposition of the remaining Kommando was as follows: crematoria 2 and 3 contained 169 each who slept in the attic; the other 325 who serviced crematoria 4, 5, and the open burning pits were housed in crematorium 4; and the Greeks were mainly in crematoria 4 and 3 with several in crematorium 2. The ghettoization of the Sonderkommando had been in effect since the end of June 1944 when Hauptscharffuehrer Moll decided to isolate it from the rest of the camp. Even so, contact via crematorium 1 was maintained with the resistance in the main camp through the ration carriers and injured prisoners who frequented the hospital.

Then the Nazis made a bold attempt to reduce the remaining Sonderkommando by half. On the Sabbath of October 7, the numbers were called of the 300 Greeks and the Hungarians who had been previously selected. At this point, according to Greek survivors, Joseph Varouh,[9] a career line officer in the Greek army, shouted for the Greeks to charge the SS. The Greek-planned revolt failed, however, when the remaining crematoria did not implement their assigned roles.[10] So the Greeks of crematoria 3 and 4 rioted, grabbed some weapons and barricaded themselves inside the building. SS reinforcements arrived and after about an hour the Greeks dynamited crematory 4 and died singing the Greek national anthem.[11] The Greeks and others in crematorium 3 were captured by the SS and executed on the spot. Within a short time, SS pursuit squads captured and killed in battle a few kilometers outside the camp the Russians who had escaped from crematorium 1. The total casualties came to about 450. Thus about two-thirds of the Kommando died in the revolt and its aftermath. A smaller group (about 30) succeeded in escaping and was later captured. They successfully obfuscated their true identity and were interned in Dachau. The prisoners of crematoria 2 and 5 did not participate in the revolt and so were spared punishment. Their task, however, was to cremate the bodies of those killed.[12]

From this synopsis, we can discern two separate plans for a revolt: the organized plan among the veteran prisoners in conjunction with the main camp resistance movement, and the spontaneous one independently planned by the Greeks and Hungarians.[13] Some of the veterans were caught up in the latter revolt and many of them died while only a few succeeded in escaping. Only by accepting a two-stage revolt (or perhaps a planned revolt and a riot) can we hope to harmonize the two different traditions that have dominated postwar historiography. The Greek role in the planning of the original revolt, which was to have been part of a general camp revolt, is attested to mainly in Greek memoirs. Since the participants had military experience it is not improbable, although the memoirs of Polish Jews and Gentiles do not mention them. The revolt at Treblinka, for example, had to wait for a line officer to supply the necessary organization and leadership to the men who were hoping to revolt. The same situation may well have developed among the Birkenau Sonderkommando, where the presence of the main organizer of an aborted August 1944 revolt, Kapo Kaminsky, who had been a colonel in the Russian army, would have answered the need. Unfortunately a Polish kapo betrayed Kaminsky, and he was shot at the beginning of August during the liquidation of the Gypsies on August 1 and 2, 1944. As for the spontaneous revolt on October 7, there is no doubt that the Greeks were intimately involved, since it was they who had been selected and they who died in the hail of SS machine-gun fire and in the rubble of the destroyed crematorium and in the massacre following the restoration of order.[14]

The revolt resulted in about 450 prisoners killed and 2 crematoria disabled. German dead and wounded were minimal. By November Himmler ordered the cessation of gassing at Auschwitz and the crematoria were destroyed over the next several months. Auschwitz was abandoned by the majority of its prisoners in January; many of them were to die on the death marches back to Germany. The Soviet army liberated the camp shortly thereafter. The psychological impact of the revolt, however, was immense on the other slaves and has become a symbol among both survivors and the scholars who continue to record their horrible experience. Apparently the revolt gave the other prisoners a boost in confidence, perhaps *mutatis mutandis* somewhat similar to the wave of Allied bombings of the camp. These showed that Nazis could be killed and that that their own fellow slaves could revolt. Perhaps such knowledge gave to some of the slaves the incentive to survive the vicissitudes of the last seven months of the war.[15]

NOTES

1. Cf. the contemporary diary of Heinz Kounio, *Ezasa ton thanaton* (Thessaloniki, 1981) for the Greeks of the Mauthausen subcamps; English translation by Marcia Haddad Ikonomopoulos, *A Liter of Soup and Sixty Grams of Bread* (New York, 2003) and Iakovos Kambanellis, *Mauthausen* (Athens, 1995) for the Greek experiences in the main camp.
2. Yoseph Ben, *Greek Jewry in the Holocaust and the Resistance 1941–1944* (Tel Aviv, 1985), devotes a chapter to their story based on 03/2598; English version in Michael Matsas, *Illusion of Safety* (New York, 1997), pp. 257–63.
3. The four men involved included Alter Fajnzylberg, a French Jew, Szlomo Dragon and his brother Jack, and a Greek Jew named Alex who actually snapped the pictures. (Alberto Errara (below) used the alias Aleko, but I am not able to verify whether he was that Alex.) The often-reproduced pictures are available with discussion in Jonathan Webber and Connie Wilsack, *Auschwitz. A History in Photographs* (Warsaw and Bloomington, IN, 1993), pp. 172 ff.

and Fajnzylberg's testimony pp. 42 f.

4. See Philip Friedman, 'Jewish Resistance to Nazism,' in *Roads to Extinction: Essays on the Holocaust*, ed. Ada June Friedman (New York, 1980), pp. 387–408.

5. See my *Agony of Greek Jewry during World War II* (forthcoming), ch. 6 for details.

6. The account of Leon Cohen was written in French during the 1970s; published in Hebrew translation in *Pe'amim* 27 (1986); and in English as *From Greece to Birkenau. The Crematorium Workers' Uprising* (Tel Aviv, 1996). That of Daniel Bennahmias was published by Rebecca Fromer, *The Holocaust Odyssey of Daniel Bennahmias, Sonderkommando* (Tuscaloosa, AL, 1993). The memoir of Mois Mizrahi of Chios was taken as oral testimony and deposited in the archives of Graetz College in Philadelphia. YIVO acquired from the Bund Archives some original registration sheets from Auschwitz (YIVO Archives S-2 87). These were the first interviews with the prisoners after their arrival and numbering and which the prisoners had to sign. Later the information was put on cards for the central filing system. Beginning with #182xxx through #182757 are listed 30 Greek Jews from Arta, Corfu, Ioannina (Yannina), Athens and other locales and a few Salonika refugees who came on the twentieth Greek transport from which 320 males were selected; the remaining deportees were gassed and then cremated. See Appendix II.

7. A number of memoirs collected by Lore Shelley, *The Union Kommando in Auschwitz. The Auschwitz Munition Factory Through the Eyes of Its Former Slave Laborers* (Lantham, MD and London, 1996) shed light on this activity. Several of the memoirs mention Greek Jews in this kommando including their tragic deaths. For one example see Hermann Langbein, *Against All Hope. Resistance in the Nazi Concentration Camps 1938–1945* (New York, 2001), p. 221. See my *Agony of Greek Jewry* for additional aid.

8. Sonderkommando memoirs written on the eve of the revolt planned for early August 1944 have been discovered in the area of the Sonderkommando. Published by the Museum at Auschwitz (*Amidst a Nightmare of Crime. Manuscripts of Members of the Sonderkommando*, 1973), they are discussed in Reuben Ainsztein, *Jewish Resistance in Nazi-occupied Eastern Europe* (London, 1974), s.v. See also Marsel Natzari, *Xroniko 1941–1945* (Thessaloniki, 1991).

Danuta Czech, *Auschwitz Chronicle* 724, lists the following distribution for the complement:

Squad 57B, crematorium 2	daily	84 prisoners
	nightly	85 prisoners
Squad 58B, crematorium 3	daily	84 prisoners
	nightly	85 prisoners
Squad 59B, crematorium 4	daily	84 prisoners
	nightly	85 prisoners
Squad 60B, crematorium 5	daily	72 prisoners
	nightly	84 prisoners
	Total	663 prisoners

9. The literature confuses him with numerous individuals named Joseph Baruch, a common enough name that has confused scholarship on this individual. The signature on his Auschwitz registration form which I located in YIVO, spells his last name as Varouh, and it is an honor to restore to history the correct form as he used it. He served as an officer in the 3rd Artillery Regiment of Corinth from 1937–1941. Among the 30 Greeks in the YIVO list were 16 other veterans and 1 Salonikan with Italian citizenship. These are listed in Appendix II along with other Greek names that have been indentified from this Sonderkommando.

10. See Fromer, *Holocaust Odyssey of Daniel Bennahmias* for details.

11. This tradition goes back to the Greek War of Independence. See Ioannis Makriyiannis, *Memoirs*, ed. and trans. Vassilis P. Koukis (Athens, 2001), *passim*.

12. For further details on the fate of these survivors see my *Agony of Greek Jewry*, ch. 6.

13. See Langbein, *Against All Hope*, pp. 285 ff.

14. See my 'Greeks in Auschwitz,' in Fromer, *Holocaust Odyssey of Daniel Bennahmias*.

15. On the fate of the surviving Sonderkommando see my *Agony of Greek Jewry*, ch. 6.

Afterword: Joseph Matsas and the Unsung Warriors

Joseph Matsas, the first historian of the Greek Jews in the *andartiko* researched and recorded some 650 fighters in the resistance. Many of these stories were based on oral interviews.

Matsas was uniquely qualified for this project which is still unpublished. Born in 1920 in the Epirote town of Ioannina, he was educated at the Alliance Israélite school there, the local Zossimes Gymnasium, and spent several years at the University of Thessaloniki. At the university he pursued studies in Greek literature and in the local Jewish community he studied Jewish sources and tradition, in particular the long tradition of Hebrew synagogue poetry (*piyyutim*). He served on the Albanian front during the war with Italy and after demobilization returned to the university. In spring 1943 ELAS recruiters, including Markos Vafiades, recruited him along with some 250 young Jews. After the war he returned to Ioannina where 163 Jews out of a prewar population of some 1,850 struggled to restore some sense of order. The community elected him as its religious leader, tour guide, resident scholar, and archivist, positions he filled until his death in 1986.[1]

There were other Jews in the mountains, including several nurses and fighters whom I and others have had the opportunity to interview. Matsas was the first to tell the story of Fanny Florentin, but there is more to the story as was learned in my interview with her and her husband that elicited new material to add to the legend that Matsas first told.

Fanny (Flora) Florentin served with the Greek Red Cross in Albania. She and her husband Leon escaped to the mountains of Paiko in March 1943 where she served as a nurse to a Jewish doctor (Dr Yanni, later killed during the civil war) and trained young village girls to be nurses' aides. During a horrendous withdrawal from a German search and destroy mission in the area of Grevena in autumn 1944, Fanny remained with her now abandoned wounded *andartes* and was captured along with Salomon Matalon. Before killing himself, their communist leader, gave her a knife, presumably to do the same; however, she was unable to do so and was captured. Fanny was taken to jail in Ioannina where she defiantly told the SS she was a Greek citizen and Jewish; she was then sent by train to Trikala and eventually to Pavlos Melos prison in Salonika. News of her arrival reached her sister Maidi through the wife of a Greek doctor, and Maidi contacted Flora's friend (a Belgian named Mrs. Riades) in the International Red Cross. (The sister was later saved by Kosta Zannas, the head of the Greek Red Cross.) According to Flora's own story, she was then abducted from Pavlos Melos by resistance members who had bribed the guards to let them in after word got out that she was to be executed.[2] Her story illustrates both the Jewish contributions to the mountain story and the opportunity for survival in the city where influential friends had the potential to save their Jewish colleagues.

Fanny's husband Leon was trained on a mortar, and recalls that he met with Greek-American Commandos at Veskoti in 1944.[3] In a combined British–American–ELAS venture, a bridge over the Aliakmon was destroyed. Later Leon refused the offer to go to officer training when he began to suspect Communist control over the *andartes*. After several 'people's trials', in one of which an old Greek rightist and a Jewish musician were condemned to be shot (about 36 voted 'yes' and 4 Jews 'no') Leon asked to be sent to the front and served at Deskati near Lamia with five or six other *andartes*. Salomon Matalon, also interviewed by this author, had fought with a mobile unit armed with heavy machine guns in Albania and was a mortar specialist with ELAS, along with Leon Florentin. They both averred using 1917 Mausers and adjusting the telemetry of their Italian mortars from American supplies.[4] Flora and Leon recalled several additional *andartes* during our interview: the fighters Chico Cohen, Morris Aji, who received a head wound during an attack on a village, and Morris Florentin (Flora's brother), who was shot in the hip at the Battle of Karyes and whose leg was saved by Dr. Lambrakis,[5] and Sabi Barsano and Morris Haim (a student medic) who voted 'no' along with Leon and Flora at the above trial.

There are numerous other stories that have already been deposited in archival depositions and occasionally published in various collections and histories.[6] Many more stories have yet to be told, in particular that of the early resistance in Salonika – many German officers were billeted in Jewish homes: the loose talk was reported to underground networks – and the *andarte* experience in Euboea (see Chapter 3). To date there has not been a systematic effort to collect and collate the stories of Jews in the Greek resistance movements and to integrate the results into the overall story of the war in Greece. Many of the participants kept quiet, either out of fear for their safety during the period of oppression in Greece or out of bitterness at their cool reception in Israel. Many others kept silent out of modesty or out of embarrassment in the face of the Holocaust experiences of their relatives, friends, and co-religionists.

It is now over half a century after the events of World War II and the subsequent civil war in Greece. The Greek government has granted amnesty to the Left, and many have returned from their various exiles in the Balkans and the Middle East to spend their declining years in the Patrida. We should look forward to the appearance of more memoirs. Indeed, a systematic effort should be undertaken to interview and record the experiences of all survivors of that tragic period in the history of modern Greece. Only in this way can the variety of noble and tragic experiences of all the Greek people be integrated into the story that future generations will absorb as integral to their identity as Greeks.

The story of the Jews of Greece, of whom only a declining remnant survives in its homeland, is replete with nobility and tragedy. Nearly nine of every ten Jews died, whether in Greece or deported to killing centers in Poland. Today the largest 'diaspora' of Greek Jews is in Israel, where survivors and resistance fighters still carry on the cultural heritage of the Greece that bore them. Smaller 'diasporas' flourish in Belgium, England, Canada, the United States, Mexico, Brazil, and Argentina alongside the thriving communities of Greek Christians in those and other countries. All of them need to be told the story of the Greek Jews and their contributions to the war lest their name and memory be lost to the record of Greek and Jewish history.

NOTES

1. See my 'Joseph Matsas and the Greek Resistance,' *Journal of the Hellenic Diaspora* 17 (1991), pp. 49–68.
2. Joseph Matsas presented the preliminary story on Fanny Florentin in his 1982 lecture. Additional information was supplied by Fanny Florentin to the author in 1990. She mentioned a Jack Capon who published a newspaper for EAM and was imprisoned in the Pavlos Melos prison and killed there. She also recalled a Jewish student named Morris Haim who fought in the mountains. He too was remembered by 'Kitsos' (see above Ch. 2).
3. This operation was part of the Allied plan called 'Noah's Ark' which was intended to harass the German retreat. These Americans most likely belonged to Group V, which was assigned to Mount Paikon for operations in northern Greece under the command of Lt. George Papazoglou. This group accounted for 5 bridges and 2 locomotives destroyed, 1,000 yards of railroad track blown up, and, 574 killed and wounded – all at the cost of 5 Americans wounded. The detailed reports of the Greek-American officer are illuminating for their remarks on the discipline and fighting efficiency of the *andartes*. Once, the *andarte* responsible for blowing up a train slept through its passage. On another occasion: 'once again the Andartes killed

themselves by going through the minefield like a herd of sheep. Instead of following us they took a short cut and got themselves killed [12] and wounded.' 'The only other casualties were 6 Andartis killed and wounded when they started shooting at each other during the looting of the train.'
4.   The American operation groups mention 81 mm and light mortars manned by *andartes*.
5.   The latter's murder in Salonika was the subject of the book and film Z.
6.   See my 'Granny, what did you do during the war?,' *Los Muestros*, 51 (June 2003), pp. 21–2.

Appendices

The list of Jews in the *andartiko* in Appendix I has been culled from a number of sources. It does not exhaust the total number of Jews who were in the mountains or even the *andartes*. I include in Appendix II the names of those Greek Jews who fought against the Nazis in Warsaw and in Auschwitz during August and October 1944. Their names are marked with W and ✿ respectively. Further research in the archives and among the declining number of survivors will undoubtedly elicit more names. Those Greek Jews who fought in the Greek army during the Italian and German campaigns and later in the Greek forces in exile remain a subject for another occasion. The orthography follows the sources (see Abbreviations) from which the names were taken and therefore occasionally differs from the way that the individual may have spelled it. (Hence some of the names may be duplicates.) The spelling of the Auschwitz group follows the signature of the individual where available rather than the scribal transliteration, which is occasionally misleading.

ABBREVIATIONS

Abatzopoulou (1999)	Theodosia-Soula Paulidou and Roudiger Bolts, eds, *Min apaleiphis pote ta ixni* (Thessaloniki, 1999) (in Greek)
Afterword	See Afterword in book
Ajm-c	Archive Joseph Matsas: French Catalogue
Ajm-ms	Archive Joseph Matsas: handwritten lists and notes
b.	brother
Ben	Joseph Ben, *Greek Jewry in the Holocaust and the Resistance 1941–1944* (Tel Aviv, 1985) (in Hebrew)
BJGS	*Bulletin of Judeo-Greek Studies*

Ch.	Refers to chapter in book
d.	daughter

Email data from Michael Cohen, Dr Maria Esformes, Annette Fromm, Gila Hadar et al., Theo Pavidis

f.	female
fr.	father
Frezis	Raphael Frezis, *I Israelitiki Koinotita Volou* (Volos, 1994 and 2002)
h.	husband
ICJ	Institute of Contemporary Jewry, Jerusalem

Interviews with daughter of Yaakov Arar, Yaakov Balestra, Moshe Besso, Matilda Bourla, Yolanda Bourla, Shmuel Cohen, Fanny and Leon Florentin, sister of Moshe Fortis, Jan Fuerst, Eli Hassid, Frederic Kakis, Eliasif Matsas, Yiannis Megas, Daisy Karasso Moshe, Yitzhak Moshe ['Kitsos'], Yomtov Moshe, Isaac Nehama, Isaac Philosof, Albert Preznalis, Baruch Shibi, Into Shimshi, Guy Stroumza, Sara Yehoshua ['Sarika'], Jewishpartisans.org

Jmg	© The Jewish Museum of Greece [name in bold (surname first) if unconfirmed by another source]
Kabelli	I. Kabelli, 'The Resistance of the Greek Jews', *YIVO* 8 (1953), 281–88
Kakis, Legacy	Frederic Kakis, *Legacy of Courage* (Bloomington, 2003)
Kew	PRO Kew Gardens, SOE files as listed
Lo nishkax	Shmuel Rafael, ed., *Lo nishkax*
Matkovski	Alexandar Matkovski, *History of the Jews in Macedonia* (Skopje, 1982)
Matsas, *Illusion*	Michael Matsas, *Illusion of Safety* (New York, Pella, 1997)
E.M. *Larisa*	Esdra Moyse, *The Jewish Community of Larisa* (Larisa, 2000) (in Greek)
Novitch	Miriam Novitch, *Le passage des barbares*
Routes of Hell	Shmuel Rafael, *Routes of Hell*
s.	son
w.	wife
Uris	Leon Uris, *The Angry Hills*
03/9812	Yad Vashem cited by file

Appendix I: Roll of Honor

JEWS WITH THE GREEK RESISTANCE

Name		Source
Armando Aaron from Kerkira	**jmg**	[Ch. 1; Matsas, *Illusion*, 291–4]
Dario (David) Aaron		
('Keravnos') of Salonika	**jmg**	[Matsas, *Illusion*, 306; 03/8894]
Henry Aaron of Kavalla		[email]
Achar Isaak	**jmg**	
Morris Aji		[Afterword]
Morris Akara (?)		[Ben, Ch. 8]
Salvator Algoussis	**jmg**	[Matsas, *Illusion*, 420]
Albertos (36th Regiment ELAS)		[photo from Agrinion via Marcel Yoel
Albertos (a second one in 36th Reg.)		[same from Marcel Yoel]
Zakinos Alhanati		[AJM-ms11; Novitch, 140; Ben, Ch. 8]
Nissim Alkalai of Didimotiho	**jmg**	[Novitch, 140; Ben, Ch. 8; Matsas, *Illusion*, 152]
Zakinos Alhanati (Jaquinos Alkanati)	**jmg**	[AJM-ms20]
Allalouf (service w/Force 133)		[Kew, HS5/398 (handwritten no #]
Albertos Allalouf of Volos	**jmg**	[Frezis, 225]
Elia Allaluf	**jmg**	[AJM-ms7; Novitch, 140; Ben, Ch. 8; Matsas, *Illusion*, 273]
Samuel Allalouf		[Introduction n.9]
Shemtov Allaluf of Salonika	**jmg**	[AJM-ms7]Kabelli; Novitch, 140; Ben, Ch. 8, Matkovski, 106]
Solon Alalouf		[AJM-C4 and ms]
Nisim Alkalai		[AJM-ms8]

Leon Amar of Halkis	**jmg**	[AJM-C65; Matsas, *Illusion*, 317]
Elias Almosninos		[*BJGS*, 12, Summer 1993, 28]
Raoul Amosnino of Salonika	**jmg**	[Matsas, *Illusion*, 325]
Joseph Amarilio		[AJM-C6]
Alberto Amarillio ('Aleko')		[Ch. 3]
Dario Amir of Volos		[AJM-ms10]
Isaac Amir of Trikala		[AJM-ms]
Julie Amir of Volos		[AJM-ms11]
Albertos Amon of Volos	**jmg**	[Matsas, *Illusion*, photos; Frezis, 225]
Victor Amon of Volos		[Frezis 2, 225]
Yaakov Arar (Harari) of Kastoria		[interview w/d and photo; Ben, Ch. 8; 03/2890]
Abraham Arditi	**jmg**	[Ch. 5; 03/2487]
Tsiako Arouh of Salonika		[AJM-ms14]
Dr Manolis (Emmanouel) Arukh	**jmg**	[Ch. 4; AJM-C10]
Asher Moshe	**jmg**	
Leo Askenazi		[AJM-C12]
Samuel Askenazi **[same as Eskenazi?]**	**jmg**	[Matsas, *Illusion*, photo, 291]
Albert Asseo		[AJM-ms]
Eli Attas		[Rivlin, *Yavan*, 37]
Mosheh (Moise) Attas of Athens		[Besso; AJM-C13]
Ino Attias	**jmg**	[Novitch, 140; Ben, Ch. 8, Matkovski, 106]
Attias from Kavalla		[Ch. 2]
Aaron Avdela of Volos	**jmg**	[AJM-ms1; Novitch, 140 **Victor-Aaron**]
Victor Avdela(s) of Volos	**jmg**	[AJM-ms1; Frezis 2, 225]
Salom Avdela(s) (b) of Volos	**jmg**	[Novitch, 140; Ben, Ch. 8; Frezis 2, 225]
Solomon Avdela s. of Shalom of Volos		[AJM-ms4]
Avraam of BEF		[AJM-C1; Ch. 2]
Jacques Avram of Kavala	**jmg**	[AJM-ms2 and 19; Novitch, 140; Ben, Ch. 8]

Azar (f.) of Volos		[AJM-C2]
Albert Azar of Volos		[AJM-C2]
Julie Azar of Volos		[AJM-C2]
William Isaac Azar of Volos	**jmg**	[Matsas, *Illusion*, 324; Frezis, 230]
Lazarus (Eliezer) Azaria ('Tripotamite')	**jmg**	[AJM-C3; Matsas, *Illusion*, 24]
Leon Azouli		[Ch. 3]
Rena Ioseph Azouz of Volos	**jmg**	[Matsas, *Illusion*, 324; Frezis 2, 225, 230]
Salvator Azouz (b) of Volos		[Frezis 1, p. 87]
David Bacolas		[AJM-C36]
Nissim Bacolas s. of Yeshua		[AJM-C37]
Salvator Bakolas of Ioannina "Sotiris"	**jmg**	[Ch. 4; AJM-C38; Matsas, *Illusion*, photo]
Tsion Bakola(s) s. of Yeshua of Ioannina		[AJM-C39; Eliasif Matsas]
Yaakov Balestra [or Valestra] of Corfu and brother		[Benny Natan; interview]
Raphael Barki [brother of Solomon]		[Matsas, *Illusion*, 102]
Solomon Barki in Athens		[Ch. 3]
See Varon		
Avraam Baron of Kavala		[AJM-ms19]
Abraam Baron of Salonika	**jmg**	[Matsas, *Illusion*, 324]
Barron		[Matsas, *Illusion*, 273]
Dr Sabi Barsano [Savi Basan?]		[Afterword; via Yolanda Bourla]
Jacob Barouh		[AJM-C47]
Iakov Barzilai	**jmg**	[Matsas, *Illusion*, 325]
Yosef Barzilai		[*Routes of Hell*]
Victor Batis s. of Bechor of Athens		[Ch. 5; AJM-C41]
Nissim Batish of Ioannina		[AJM-C44]
Koutiel Yakov Begas of Larisa	**jmg**	[EMoyse, *Xronika; lo nishkax*, 16, 36]
Beïs of Salonika		[AJM-C45 and ms]
Bekos		[AJM-ms]
Betsalel Behar	**jmg**	[Novitch, 140; Ben, ch. 8;]

Jacques (Zhak) Behar		[Ch. 4; Novitch, 140]
Beja see Beza		
Moshe (Morris) Bel(l)o ('Maliaropoulos')		[Ch. 2; AJM-C40]
Belevy (female)	jmg	[Novitch, 140; Matsas, *Illusion*, 108; Ben, ch. 8]
Bellelis see Vellelis		[AJM-ms - Ben Levi]
Mrs Mario Benarojia of the United States		[Matsas, *Illusion*, 324] Pepo Ben Ouzilio [Rivlin, *Yavan*, 37]
Ben Porat and two brothers	jmg	[Novitch, 141; Ben, Ch. 8; Matsas, *Illusion*, 305]
Doctor Alberto Benroubi of Salonika		[Yannis Megas]
Hayyim Ben Roubi		[Rivlin, *Yavan*, 37]
Morris Benroubi	jmg	[Matsas, *Illusion*, 325]
Menahem Bension of Kavala	jmg	[Matsas, *Illusion*, 324 **?forced labor**
Benveniste from Kavalla		[Novitch, 141 [Ben, Ch. 8, Matkovski, 106; AJM-ms]
Albert[o] Benvenista/i	jmg	[Novitch, 141; Ben, Ch. 8, Matkovski, 106]
Benjamin Benveniste	jmg	[Matsas, *Illusion*, 325]
Dick Benveniste	jmg	[Novitch, 141; Ben, Ch. 8; Matsas, *Illusion*, 291]
David Benveniste	jmg	Novitch, 141; Ben, Ch. 8, Matkovski, 106]
Esther Benveniste of Larisa		[VT-1922]
Jack (!) Benveniste		[Ch. 1]
Moshe Benveniste		[Kitsos]
Salvatore Ben Yaish		[Ch. 1]
Benjamin [killed at Agia Triada]		[Ch. 4]
Jacob (Jacaques) Israel Beraha	jmg	[EMoyse, *Xronika*] [jewish-partisans.org]
Vital Beraha of Salonika	jmg	[AJM-C48; Matsas, *Illusion*, 324]
Yehuda Beraha		[AJM-ms; Novitch, 140; Yehudit in Ben, Ch. 8]

Mentesh Besantsi		[Kabelli, Ben, ch. 8]
Moshe Besso of Athens ('Aspros')		[interview]
George Beza (Force 133 agent)		[Kew, HS5/646]
Johny Beza (w/English)	jmg	[p.xxivn; Novitch, 140; Ben, Ch. 8]
Albertos Beza	jmg	[AJM-ms; Novitch, 140]
Alfred Beza of Salonika	jmg	[Matsas, *Illusion*, 324; Ben, Ch. 8]
Helen Beza of Salonika	jmg	[Matsas, *Illusion*, 324]
Jacqueline Beza (wife of Mario Brener)	jmg	[Matsas, *Illusion*, 324]
Monika Beza of Salonika	jmg	[Matsas, *Illusion*, 324]
Yaakov Bochoropoulos s. of Israel of Ioannina		[AJM-C46]
Marcos Boton		[AJM-C52]
Salomon Bouri	jmg	
Abraam Bourla s. of Joseph of Salonika	jmg	[AJM-ms; Novitch, 141; Matsas, *Illusion*,273]
Dora Bourla 'Tarzan' of Salonika d.	jmg	[Ch. 1; Novitch, 141]
Leon Bourla 'o geros' of Salonika f.	jmg	[Ch. 1; AJM-C49]
Morice Bourla		[AJM-C50]
Mois(sis) (Moshe) Bourla(s) of Salonika	jmg	[Ch. 1; Matsas, *Illusion*, 325]
Nikos Bourla of Salonika	jmg	[AJM-C51; Matsas, *Illusion*, 273, 324]
Sarika Bourla of Veria		
Solomon (Charles) Bourla of Salonika (2)	jmg	[Ch. 1]
Tselebe Bourla of Serrai	jmg	[AJM-ms; Matsas, *Illusion*, 273]
Yitshak (Isaac) Bourla		[Novitch, 141; Ben, Ch. 8]
Yolanda Bourla d. of Leon of Salonika	jmg	[Ch. 1; Novitch, 141; Ben, Ch.8]
Yosef Bourla		[Ben, Ch. 8]

Roverto Brellis
  (poet and doctor)   **jmg** [EMoyse, *Xronika*]
David Broudo of Salonika   **jmg** [Ch. 4; Matsas, *Illusion*, 325]
Michel Broudo of Salonika [b] **jmg** [Novitch, 141; Ben, Ch. 8,
                                  Matkovski, 106]

Mimis Cabelis of Trikala   **jmg**
Jack Capon   [Afterword]
Matilda Capon (mar. Moshe Bourla)
  'Mondos'   [interview]
Charles Caras of Salonika   **jmg** [Matsas, *Illusion*, 324]
See also Karasso
Alberto Carasso of Salonika   **jmg** [AJM-ms; Novitch, 141; Ben,
                                Ch. 8, Matsas, *Illusion*, 272]

Betty Carasso (s of Marco and Daisy) [03/5867]
Charles Carasso of Salonika **jmg** [AJM-C95;Matsas, *Illusion*,
                                273, 305]

Daisy Carasso of Salonika   **jmg** [Ch. 3]
Emmanuel Carasso   **jmg** [Novitch, 141;Ben, Ch. 8]
Marco Alberto Carasso of
  Salonika b. of Daisy   **jmg** [Ch. 3; Novitch, 141; Ben,
                                Ch. 8; Matsas, *Illusion*, 303]

Yosef Carasso   [Ben, Ch. 8]
Zhak Carasso   [Ben, Ch. 8]
Carlos of Salonika   **jmg** [Ben, p. 127, Matsas, *Illusion*,
                                307; 03/8894]

Caron Jacques [Capon?] **jmg**
Rabbi Cassouto of Larissa **(jmg)** [Novitch, 141]
Yitshak Cassuto   [Ben, Ch. 8]
Saltiel Cattegno of Salonika
  and brother   [Matsas, *Illusion*, 289]
Jacques Catan   **jmg** [Novitch, 142;Matsas,
                                Illusion, 291]

Maurice Cazes   [Introduction n.9]
Isac Chanen ('Sophianos')   [Ch. 3]
See Cohen, Coen, Kohen, Koen
Albert Coen of Ioannina ('Vladimir') [AJM-C74; EMoyse, *Xronika*]]
Davico Coen s. of Michael   [AJM-C75]
Coen of Chalkis (Kapetan Kronos)
  See Louis!   [AJM-C78]
Aharon Cohen of Athens

[brother Mosheh]   [Besso]

Albert Cohen of Drama   **jmg**   [Novitch, 142; Ben, Ch. 8, Matkovski, 106]

Dr Albert Cohen ('Vladamir') **jmg** [Ch. 4]

Anna S. Cohen of Volos   **jmg**   [Frizis 2, 226; EMoyse, *Xronika*]

Barukh Cohen of Volos   [interview w/Shmuel Cohen]

Boby (Robby/Robi/Rubi)

  Samuel Cohen   **jmg**   [Novitch, 142; Ben, Ch. 8; Matsas, *Illusion*, 287; Matkovski, 106]

Dario Cohen of Volos   [interview w/Shmuel Cohen]

David Cohen   [Ch. 2; Novitch, 142; Ben, Ch. 8, Matkovski, 106]

David Michael Cohen

  of Preveza   **jmg**   [Matsas, *Illusion*, 273] exec. in Athens or mts?

David Shabbetai Cohen   **jmg**   [Novitch, 142; Ben, Ch. 8]

Eli Cohen   [Ch. 2; Novitch, 142; Ben, Ch.8]

Elias Youda Cohen of Larisa   [Novitch, 142; E.M., *Larisa*]

Elias Cohen of Salonika   **jmg**   [Matsas, *Illusion*, 324]

Hayyim ('Chico') Cohen   [Ch. 2; Novitch, 142?]

Hayyim Samuel Cohen

  of Volos   **[jmg]** [Novitch, 142; Ben, Ch. 8; 03/8664; Frezis 2, 226]

Iakov Cohen of Volos   [Frezis 2, 231]

Ilias Coen s. of Nissim   [AJM-C81]

Isaak (Jacques) Cohen

  of Volos   **jmg**   [Matsas, *Illusion*, 272; Kabelli; Novitch, 142; Ben, 130; Frezis 2, 231]

Jacob Cohen of Volos   **jmg**   [AJM-ms; Novitch, 142]

Joseph Avraam Coen of Ioannina [AJM-C79]

Joseph Coen ('Tsitos')   [AJM-C80]

Karolina Cohen of Volos   [Frezis 2, 231]

Laura Cohen   [jewishpartisans.org]

Leon Cohen of Athens   [Matsas, *Illusion*, 182]

Leon Ioseph Cohen of Volos **jmg** [Matsas, *Illusion*, 324; Frizis
                                     2, 230]

Louis Cohen ('Kronos')
  of Xanthi   **jmg** [Ch. 4]
Maurice Cohen b. of Tsitos   **jmg** [AJM-C80]
Menachem Cohen   **jmg** [Matsas, *Illusion*, 288]
Menasche Cohen   [AJM-C82; Novitch, 142;
                                      Ben, Ch. 8]

Michael Elias Cohen
  of Ioannina   **jmg** [AJM-C83; Matsas, *Illusion*,
                                      198; interview]

Morris (Moshe) Cohen s.
  of Haim Moissis   **jmg** [Chs. 2, 5;AJM-ms; Novitch,
                                      142; Ben, Ch. 8, Matkovski,
                                      109]

Moshe Cohen of Athens
  [b. of Aharon]   [Besso]
Moshe Coen of Kavala   [AJM-C84]
Nissim Cohen of Volos   **jmg** [AJM-ms; Novitch, 142; Ben,
                                      Ch. 8, Matkovski, 109; Frezis 2,
                                      226]

Pepos Cohen of Volos   **jmg** [Matsas, *Illusion*, photos; R.
                                      Frezis 2, 225]

Pinhas Cohen from Florina   [Ch.   1]
Rachel Cohen of Volos   **jmg** [Frizis, *Volos*; [EMoyse,
                                      Xronika]

Rozita Cohen of Volos
  (d. of Hayyim)   **jmg** [Frizis *Volos*; 03/8664;
                                      EMoyse, *Xronika*]

Rosa Cohen of Salonika   [Ch. 2; AJM-C174]
Sabbethai Cohen
  of Volos [EPON]   **jmg** [Frezis 2, p. 231]
Salvator Cohen
  of Volos [EPON]   **jmg** [AJM-C85;Novitch, 142; Ben,
                                      Ch. 8; Matsas, *Illusion*, 324,
                                      Frezis 2, 226, 230]

Sam Cohen of Salonika   [interview 4/4/03]
Samouel Coen s. of Aaron
  ('Balomenos')   [AJM-C86]

Samuel Cohen of Ioannina   **jmg**   [Matsas, *Illusion*, 198, 310; Eliasif Matsas]

Samuel [Shmuel] Cohen of Volos   [Matsas, *Illusion*, 32; via Shmuel Cohen; Frezis, 230]

Shimon Cohen of Volos   [interview w/Shmuel Cohen]
Simon Cohen of Athens   **jmg**   [Kabelli]
Shlomo Cohen of Volos
Solomon Coen s. of Avraam
  of Ioannina   AJM-C87]
Stella Cohen of Salonika EPON **jmg**   [AJM-C88; Matsas, *Illusion*, 324; Abatzopoulou,1999, 117]

Viktor Cohen son of Zhak
  of Volos   [Kabelli, Ben, 130]
Yehoshua Cohen   [AJM-C89; Ben, Ch. 8]
Yeshua Cohen   **jmg**   [AJM-C89; Novitch, 142; Matsas, *Illusion*, 288]

Yaakov Cohen   [Ben, ch. 8][
Yitshak Cohen [same as Kroniko?]   [Ben, Ch. 8]
Yitshak Cohen ('Kroniko')
  of Xanthi   **jmg**   [Ch. 4]
Yosef Cohen from Florina "Tarzan" [Ch. 1; *lo nishkax*, 18, 22
  [b. Pinhas]   "Viliptari"]
Zaharias Cohen of Volos   **jmg**   [Ch. 2; Matsas, *Illusion*, 325; Frezis, 230]

Zouli Cohen (Julie) of Volos **jmg**   [Frizis 1, p. 90]
Tori Cuenka   **jmg**   [Novitch, 142; Ben, Ch. 8; Matkovski, 106 – Kenka,]

Ieremias Daniel with EDES   [photo via Michael Matsas]
David (?)   **jmg**
Dariko who played the accordion   [Ch. 2]
Isaac Dassa (Ntassa)   [AJM-C148]
Vital Dasa   **jmg**   [Matsas, *Illusion*, p. 325]
Iossif David   [AJM-C25]
Mimis David   [AJM-C26]
Samouel David   [AJM-C66]
Iosif Decastro of Hania   **jmg**   [Matsas, *Illusion*, p. 325]
Marcel DeMayo of Bitola   [Matkovski, p. 106; 03/6313]
Samuel Dentis of Arta   **jmg**   [AJM-C27;Matsas, *Illusion*, p.

		324 of Hania; Besso]
Ovadia Dino		[AJM-ms]
...Eliahu　　(h of Dorika Raban)		[03/9812]
Misel Elias of Volos		[Frezis 2, 226]
Ilias Eliassif　b of Victor		[AJM-C29]
Victor Eliassif		[AJM-C28]
Isaac Eliezer of Agrinion	**jmg**	[Matsas, *Illusion*, 307; Tziako AJM-C29(!)]
Dr Eliezer		[AJM-C30]
s. of Dr Eliezer		[AJM-C31]
Isaak Emanuel		[ch. 2; AJM-C34; Novitch, 142; Ben, ch. 8, Matkovski, 106]
Elias Errera		[AJM-C32]
Moris (Maurice) Errera of Salonika	**jmg**	[AJM-ms; Novitch, 142; Matkovski, 106]
Morris Esformes of Salonika		[via daughter Dr Maria E]
Mois Eskaloni		[email]
Leon Eskenazi f. of Alberto		[AJM-C32(!)]
Samuel Eskenazi s. of Moisi of Larisa		[Ch. 5; P interview; E.M., *Larisa*; AJM-C33]
David Ezra s. of Marcos of Karditsa		[AJM-C63 and ms16]
Chaim Ezra s. of Besso		[AJM-C65]
Maurice Ezra s. of Besso		[AJM-C64]
Albert Ezrati		[AJM-C35]
Avraam Felous of Trikala		[AJM-C53]
Allegra Felous of Trikala		[Abatzopoulou, 1999, 117]
Chryssoula Felous d. of Avraam of Trikala /Volos	**jmg**	[AJM-C56; Matsas, *Illusion*, 324; Frezis 2, 230]
Elias Felous		[AJM-C35]
Jacce (Jacob) Felous		[AJM-C5
Markos Felous of Volos/Athens**jmg**		[Sarika; Frezis 2, 226]
Albertos Feretzi	**jmg**	[Matsas, *Illusion*, 420]
Moissi Feretzi	**jmg**	[Matsas, *Illusion*, 420]
Sadon Feretzi	**jmg**	[Matsas, *Illusion*, 420]
Martha Fischmann of Athens (serv Force 133)		[Kew, HS5/398 #635]

Victoria Fischmann of Athens
(serv Force 133)   [Kew, HS5/398 #636]
Fanny Florentin/Matalon   **jmg** [Afterword, Matsas, *Illusion*,
(aka Matilda)   308, 313; interviw]
Morris Florentin   [Afterword]
Aaron Fornia of Chalkis   [Sarika]
Abram[ino] Fornis of Halkis   **jmg** [AJM-C58;Matsas, *Illusion*,
                                                           317]

Moissis (Mosheh) (Mimi)
   Fortis ['Byron']   [03/5826; interview with s.]
Pepo (Yosef) Fortis   [03/5826]
Simon Fraggis s. of Jacob
   of Salonika   **jmg** [Matsas, *Illusion*, 324; Sarika;
                                                           AJM-ms- **Frangis**]
Frizis of Salonika   [Matsas, *Illusion*, 274, 324]
Albert Franies
   of Larisa   **[Francis   jmg]** [Matsas, *Illusion*, 325]
Manolis Frangis of Chalkis   **jmg** [Sarika]
Manolis Franzis of Volos   [Frezis 2, 226]
Raoul Frangis   **jmg** [Novitch, 142 ; Matkovski,
                                                           106 ; Sarika]

(Raoul Francis)   [I. Frizis, 22]
Avraam-Chaim Frezis
   of Chalkis   **jmg** [Sarika]
Jacob Frizis of Salonika   [AJM-C60, C61]
Frizis of Volos   [AJM-C62]
Karmen Frezis of Volos   **jmg** [Frezis 2, 226]
Raphael A. Frezis of Volos
[br of K.F   **jmg** [Sarika; Frezis 2, 226]
Fredzi   **[See Feretzi]**   [Matsas, *Illusion*, 307;
                                                           03/8894]

Jan (Jacob) Fuerst from Poland   [Ch. 1; Novitch, 143; Ben, ch.
                                                           8; interview]

Ganis Daron   **jmg**
Marko Ganis of Larisa   [AJM-ms16; Matsas, *Illusion*,
                                                           278]

Mordos Yosif Ganis of Larisa   [E.M., *Larisa*]
Solomon Ganis of Agrinion   **jmg** [AJM-ms17; Novitch, 143;
                                                           Ben, Ch. 8]

Solon Ganis of Volos   [Frezis 2, 225]
David Gatenio of Salonika EPON   [Abatzopoulou, 1999, 118]

Joseph Gategno of Salonika	jmg	[AJM-C22]
Saltiel Gategno [see Cattegno]		[AJM-C22(!);Ben, Ch. 8]
Gavrielides of Ioannina		[Michael Cohen]
Albert Gavrielides s. of Samuel		[AJM-ms25]
Samuel Leon Gavrielides		
of Athens	jmg	[AJM-C17;Matsas, *Illusion*, 274]
Jacob Gerson of Ioannina	jmg	[AJM-C24; Matsas, *Illusion*, p. 198, 315; Eliasif Matsas]
Grotas		[AJM-C23]
David Hacohen		[Ben, ch. 8; Ch. 4]
Solon Hadjis of Volos		[AJM-C70]
Yohanas (Johanan) Hadjis		
('Skoufas') of Arta	jmg	[Ch. 5; AJM-C69; Ben, Ch. 8]
Iliya Hakim of Larisa		[Ph interview]
Menahem Haham (Hatzopoulos)		[AJM-C71]
Zeev Hakla'i of Palestine		[Haklai, *With Russian POWs*]
Raoul Halvadji		[AJM-C68]
Benjamin Hamami of 2 coy		
AMPC 'Hanti' ('Alexo')		[Kew, H5/521]
Hayyim Hanokh of Salonika		
[in Athens]		[03/3215]
Yehuda Harari of Kastoria		
[see Arrar]		[Ben, Ch. 8; 03/2890]
Eli Hassid of Salonika [in Evvoia]		[interview]
Yosef Hassid of Salonika [in Evvoia]		[above interview; 03/11121 b of Hector?]
Avraham Hasson "Barbadavas"		[AJM-ms]
Moise Hasson s. of Savas		
[same as Moissis?]		[AJM-C73]
Moissis Hasson of Salonika	jmg	[Matsas, *Illusion*, 324]
Pepo Hasson of Bitola		[Matkovski, 106
Sabas Hasson of Salonika	jmg	[AJM-C72 and ms; Matsas
(Savas Sabbas)		*Illusion*, 324]
Shabtai Hasson		[Ch. 2]
Apostolos Hatzopoulos	jmg	Matsas, *Illusion*, 308
Minas Hatzopoulos		

of Ioannina	**jmg**	[Matsas, *Illusion*, 198]
Morris Hayyim	[**Haim** -jmg**	[Ch. 2; Novitch, 143; Ben, ch. 8, Matkovski, 106;

[Dr Maurice Haim in AJM-ms but he was a pre-med student]

Theodore Hirshhorn from Vienna		[Ch. 1]
Nathan Honen of Kastoria		[033C/3796]
Haim Iakovou of Volos		[Frezis 1, 87]
Sabbas Iakovou (b) tou Semou & Rebekkas of Volos		[Frezis 1, 87, 89]
Leon Idis [or Idas]		[jewish partisans.org]
Alberto Iessoulas of Volos	**jmg**	[Frezis 2, 225]
Moissis Elia Iessoulas of Volos	**jmg**	[Frezis 2, 230]
Luna Ishak of Bitola		[Matkovski, 106]
Mentesh Ishak of Bitola		[Matkovski, 106]
Pekho Ishak of Bitola		[Matkovski, 106]
Yoseph Issis (Izis)	**jmg**	[*lo nishkax*, 16,36; EMoyse, *Xronika*]
Savvas Issis s. of Efraim of Art	**jmg**	[AJM-C67; Matsas, *Illusion*, 324]
Jacques Chaim	**jmg**	
Matika Kabeli of Trikkala	**jmg**	[Matsas, *Illusion*, 324]
Albert Kakis		[Kakis, *Legacy*]
Carmen Kakis		[Ch. 3; YM interview; Kakis, *Legacy*]
Emil Kakis (father) of Drama		[Kakis, *Legacy*]
Frederic Kakis		[Kakis, *Legacy*]
Zack Kakis		[Kakis, *Legacy*]
Kalderon of Florina (2 brothers)		[03/11552]
David Kalderan of Bitola		[Matkovski, 106]
Charlo Kalderon of Bitola (b of Gita)		[03/6313]
Gita Kalderon of Bitola		[03/6313]
Julie Kalderon	**jmg**	[Frezis 2, 226]
Luna Kalderon of Bitola (s of Gita)		[03/6313]
Samuel Kalderan of Bitola		[Matkovski, 106]
Avraam Kalefezra of Ioannina		[AJM-C91]
Alekos Kalefezra b. of Avraam		[AJM-C92]
Moise Kamhi of Salonika		[email]
Moissis Kamhis of Larissa		[interview w/Shmuel Cohen]

Nissim Kamhi		[AJM-ms; Novitch, 143]
Alegra Kapetas		[AJM-C93]
Elias Kapetas of Trikkala	**jmg**	[Matsas, *Illusion*, 325; Esdra Moyse]
Elias Kapetas of Volos	same?)	[Frezis 2, 226]
Kapetas Yahiel	**jmg**	
Solomon Kapetas	**jmg**	[AJM-C94; Matsas, *Illusion*, 325]

Avraam Alberto Karasso
  of Salonika ('Aleko')   [granddaughter]
Daniel Karasso   (I. Frizi, 22]
Moise Karasso   **jmg**   [AJM-ms]
Tziako Karasso (w/ Kapitan Zoulas) [AJM-C96]
Karol Karasso   [EMoyse, *Xronika*]
Albert Kasorla of Bitola   [Matkovski, 106]
Solomon Kastro tou David of Volos [Frezis 2, 226, 230]
Aris Kazis ('Kolokotrone')   [Ch. 5]
Shmuel Kazes of Komotini   [interview]
Nissim Kimhi **[Kamhi/s]**   **jmg**   [Ben, Ch. 8, Matkovski, 106]
Joseph Koen (Konen) of Crete   [Ch. 1; *BJGS* 13, 32]
Solon Komidis of Komotini
  [from Limnos]   [interview w/Shmuel Cohen]
Elias Kones of Volos   **jmg**   [Matsas, *Illusion*, 289; Frezis, *Volos*; 03/8664]

Mishel Kone of Volos (b)   **jmg**   [Frezis 1, 87]
Moissis Kones of Volos   **jmg**   [Frezis 2, 226]
Isaac (Zak) Kostis   **jmg**   [Ch. 6; book; AJM-C97]
Yaakov (Jacob) Koumeri
  [in Chicago?]   [Yomtov Moshe; AJM-98]
Kounio, b. of Sarah Kounio,
  a pharmacist?   [Ch. 2; AJM-C99]
Joseph Lahanas of Arta   **jmg**   [Matsas, *Illusion*, 274]
Alberto Lazar   [AJM-ms]
Isaac Lazar   [Ch. 2;AJM-ms]
Lazaros Lazar b. of Isaac   [AJM-ms]
Nissim Lazar   [AJM-ms]
Salvator Lazar   [Ch. 2]

Aaron Levi of Trikala		[AJM-C100]
Abraham Levi of Chalkida		[AJM-ms]
Abraham Levy of Salonika		
[**Levi Avraam**	**jmg]**	AJM-C101; Novitch, 143; Kabelli, Ben, Ch. 8]
Chaim Leon Levi of Ioannina	**jmg**	[Matsas, *Illusion*,273]
Elias Levi of Trikala	**jmg**	[*lo nishkax*, 16,37]
Eliahu Levy of Athens	**jmg**	[AJM-C102; Novitch, 143; Kabelli, Ben, Ch. 8]
Emmanuel Levy of Athens	**jmg**	[AJM-C103; Novitch, 143; Kabelli, Ben, Ch. 8]
Dr. Errikos Levy of Ioannina		
[**Levi**]	**jmg**	[Ch. 1]
Haim Levi s. of Leon of Ioannina		[AJM-C106]
Jacques Levi ("Perakles") of Salonika		[Guy Stroumza's uncle; AJM-C105]
Kaity Levi of Trikkala	**jmg**	[Matsas, *Illusion*, 217]
Manolis Levi b. in law of "Perikles"		[AJM-ms]
Matathias Levi s. of Victor		[AJM-C107]
Meir Levi of Trikala ("Agronos")		[AJM-C108; *lo nishkax*, 16,37; Matsas, *Illusion*, 320]
Levi Moissis	**jmg**	**[Lt. Killed by Germans trying to escape?]**
Neino Levi		[AJM-C109]
Ovadia Levi		AJM-C110]
Rosa Levi		[AJM-C111]
Rula or Rahel Levi, wife of 'Perikles'		[Ch. 2]
Shimon Levi s. of Moisi		
of Larisa	**jmg**	[Novitch, 143; Ben, Ch. 8 AJM-C112; E. M. *Larisa*; Monument at Karalaka]
Solomon Abraam Levi		
of Trikala	**jmg**	[Matsas, *Illusion*, 217, 274]
Solon Avraam Levi	**jmg**	[AJM-ms]
Jacques (Ya'akov) Levi ('Perikles')		[Ch. 2]
Zacharia Levi		[AJM-ms]
David H. Levis of Volos	**jmg**	[AJM-C104 ; Frezis 2, 226,229; EMoyse, *Xronika*]

Elias Levis of Trikala		[EMoyse, *Xronika*]
Meyer Levis of Trikala	jmg	Matsas, *Illusion*, 320, 324; [EMoyse, *Xronika*]
Moissis Levis of Volos		[Frezis 2, 226, 228]
Nellos Levis of Volos	jmg	[Frezis 2, 226]
Zahos Levis of Volos	jmg	[Frezis 2, 226]
Yakov Magrizos s. of Moisi of Larisa	jmg	[Novitch, 143; Ben, ch. 8; E.M., *Larisa*; Monument at Karalaka]
Simantov Maissi	jmg	[Matsas, *Illusion*, 420]
Raphael Maltas		[Ch. 5]
Raoul Mano	jmg	[Matsas, *Illusion*, 290]
Rachel Mano		[AJM-C115]
Clemy Margos of (Cairo) Athens		[Rinette Margosh Seidner of Houston]
Walter Margos of (Cairo) Athens		[Rinette Margosh Seidner of Houston]
Matilda Massarano		[Eli Pinhas; picture in Salonika Museum]
Isaak Massot	jmg	[Matsas, *Illusion*, 305]
Fani Florentin/Matalon w. of Leon		[AJM-C117; **See Florentin**]
Leon Matalon	jmg	[Afterword; AJM-C116; Matsas, *Illusion*, 308]
Salomon Matalon		[Afterword]
Matilde Matarasso of Salonika		[AJM-C118]
Moissis/Mosheh Matathias of Volos	jmg	[AJM-C114; interview w/ Shmuel Cohen, Frezis, 228]
Zacko Matathias of Volos [f of M.M.]		[interview w/Shmuel Cohen]
Nissim Matityahu (Matathias?) [?of Corfu]		[03/4273] in Auschwitz, etc.]
Chaim Matsas of Ioannina	jmg	[AJM-C121; Matsas, *Illusion*, 310]
Eliasif Matsas of Ioannina	jmg	[AJM-C119; Matsas, *Illusion*, 198; interview]
Joseph Matsas s of Menahem of Ioannina		[Ch. 1; AJM-C122]
Mois Matsas		[AJM-C124]

Pappas Matsas   [AJM-C113]
Solomon Matsas s of Menahem
  of Ioannina   [AJM-C123;Matsas, *Illusion*,
                                    199]
Yeshua Matsas of Ioannina   jmg   [AJM-C120; Matsas, *Illusion*,
  [b of Eliasif]   198; Eliasif Matsas]
Shlomo Matsil of (Ioannina) Preveza [Ch. 5]
Leon Meir   [Ch. 5]
Avraam Mevorach of Kavala   [AJM-C130]
Samuel Meyir of Ioannina   jmg   AJM-C129; Matsas, *Illusion*,
                                    200]
Avraam Michael of Ioannina   [AJM-C137]
Alberto Moses Minervo of Hania
  [Agent G-4]   jmg   [AJM-C142; Matsas, *Illusion*,
                                    159; EMoyse, *Xronika*]
Jenny Minervos in Crete   jmg
Salvator Minervos of Hania   jmg   [Matsas, *Illusion*, 325]
Miyoni of Agrinion   [AJM-C128]
Yonas Mi(y)onis of Agrinion   jmg   [AJM-C126;Matsas, *Illusion*,
                                    325; Ch. 2]
Miskatel brothers of Didimotiho   [Matsas, *Illusion*, 153]
Mitrani (poet)   [I. Frizi, 22]
Lili Mitrani of Salonika   [Ch. 3]
Robert Mitranis ('Hippokrates')
  of Serres   jmg   [Ch. 4]
Moshe Miyuni (Moissis -   jmg   [Ch. 2; AJM-C127; Matsas
  Miyonis] of Ioannina   *Illusion*, 198]
aka Moshe 'Katsapas'   jmg   [Matsas, *Illusion*, 316]
Mizan   jmg   Novitch, 143; Ben, Ch. 8]
David Mizan of Drama   jmg   [Novitch, 143; Ben, Ch. 8,
                                    Matkovski, 106]
Ilias Mizan   [AJM-C131]
Isaac Mizan of Agrinion   jmg   [AJM-C132; Ben, ch. 8]
Jacob Mizan   [AJM-C133]
Leon Mizan   jmg   [AJM-C134; Novitch, 143;
                                    Ben, Ch. 8]
Sabetai Mizan   [AJM-C136]
Sami Mizan of Larisa   [P. interview; AJM-C135]

Saul Mizan of Bulgaria		[Arditi]
Zakino Mizan of Volos	jmg	[Ben, Ch. 8; Frezis 2, 226]
Alberto Mizrahi of Larisa		[Ph interview]
Haim Misrahis of Volos		[Frezis 2, 226]
Minas Mizrachi of Volos	jmg	[Frezis 2, 226]
Sarina Mizrachi of Volos	jmg	[Frezis 2, 226]
Zak Mizrahis of Volos		[Frezis 2, 226]
Yosef Mizrahi [EAM] of Athens		[interview with widow]
Elio Modiano (son of Sam M)		[ICJ #4 (146)]
Sam Modiano of Salonika	jmg	[Kabelli, Ch. 6; ICJ #4 (146)]
Albertos (Avraam) Moissis		
of Volos	jmg	[Frezis 2, 231]
Asher Moissis of Trikala/Athens		[Ch. 6]
Esdras Beniamin Moisis of Larisa		[E.M., *Larisa*]
David Moissis	jmg	[Matsas, *Illusion*, 325]
Hason Moissis ben Sabba		[AJM-ms]
Molho	jmg	[Matsas, *Illusion*, 274]
A. Molho ('Napoleon')	jmg	[Kabelli; Novitch, 143; Ben,
of Salonika		Ch. 8, Matkovski, 106]
Sophie Moltiah		[Ben, Ch. 8]
Morris or Maurice		[03/9812]
Moisis (Moshe) Mordos		
of Volos	jmg	[Frezis 2, 226]
Mordoch	jmg	[AJM-C140; Matsas, *Illusion*,
		273]
Moskovitis of Drama [Col. at HQ]		[Kakis, *Legacy*, 221]
Moschovitz Menty (Medi)	**jmg**	[AJM- C141]
[teacher killed in Euvoia: Sarika]		
Moshe and his father		[Ben, 127, Matsas, *Illusion*,
		307]
Yitshak Mosheh ('Kitsos')		
of Salonika	jmg	[Ch. 2; interview; AJM-C138]
Yomtov Mosheh (Malias)		
of Ioannina	jmg	[Ch. 4; interview; AJM-C20]
Anselm Mourtzoukos		
(s of Leon)	jmg	[Isaac Nehama; Frezis 2, 226]
Aliki Mourtzoukou (d of Leon)	jmg	[Isaac Nehama; Frezis 2, 226]

Dr. Ernst Myller of Athens		[Ch. 6; interview with Liselotte Myller]
Col. Eddie Myers [BLO] of G. B.		[*Agony*, Ch. 8; interview]
Nahmias of Florina (several brothers?)		[03/11552]
David Nahmias of Larisa		[Ch. 1; interview w/Shmuel Cohen]]
Sam Nahmias of Athens		[Ch. 6]
Ilias Nahoum s. of Bechor of Ioannina		[AJM-C143]
Shlomo Nahum [?]		[niece Deganit Eliakim of Haifa U]
Marsel Natzari		[*Chroniko 1941–1945* (Thessaloniki, 1991)]
Albert Negrin of Trikala		[Ch. 1; interview]
Benjamin Negrin of Trikala, ('Maios' or 'Gaies')	jmg	[Ch. 1;AJM-C144; Ben, Ch. 8; Matsas, *Illusion*, 294]
Isaac Negrin of Trikala		[AJM-C146]
Dr Michael Negrin of Athens	jmg	[AJM-C145; Matsas, *Illusion*, 298–301]
Isaac Nehama from Athens		[Ch. 1; interview]
Joseph Nehama		[Ch. 6]
Jacques (Zhak) Nissan	jmg	[Novitch, 143; Ben, Ch. 8; Matsas, *Illusion*, 288]
Roel Nissahon		[Ch. 2]
Elias Sam Nissim of Salonika	jmg	[Ch. 1]
Solomon Nissim	jmg	[Ben, Ch. 8]
Yoel Nitsahon of Trikala		[AJM-C147]
Isidore Noah (Kapetan Sidris)		[Ch. 1]
Paul Noah		[Ch. 1]
(and their two brothers)		[Ch. 1]
Avraam Ovadias of Volos		[Frezis 2, 226]
Danny (Deno) Ovadia[s] of Salonika	jmg	[Ch. 2;AJM-C149; Matsas, *Illusion*, 324]
Isak Ovadia from Czechoslovakia		[Ch. 2]
Isaak Ovadias Iosef		[Monument at Karalaka]
Minos Ovadia[s] of Volos	jmg	[AJM-C150; Novitch, 143; Ben, Ch. 8]
Salvator Ovadias of Salonika	jmg	[AJM-C151; Matsas, *Illusion*,

p. 325]

Albertos Yosif Ovvadias	jmg	[E.M., *Larisa*]
Barron Pardo of Kavalla	jmg	[Matsas, *Illusion*, 273]
Mois Pardo of Kavalla	jmg	[Matsas, *Illusion*, 273]
Savvas Pardo of Kavalla	jmg	[Matsas, *Illusion*, 273]
"Parisalides" from Drama		[AJM-C152 and ms]
Raul Parnassos		[Ben, Ch. 8]
Anya Patchnik of Vienna (EPON)		[03/9922]
Harry Patchnik of Vienna		[03/9922]
Avram Peles		[AJM-ms]
Joseph Pepo of Athens	jmg	[EMoyse, *Xronika*]
Perahia of Salonika		[AJM-ms]
P. Perahia		[AJM-C153]
Flora Perahia of Salonika	jmg	[AJM-C154;Matsas, *Illusion*, 324]
Yitzhak Persky of Palestine	jmg	[Matsas, *Illusion*, 320]
Baruh Pesondes		[AJM]
Allegra Pessah	jmg	[Frezis 2, 231]
David Pessah [b&s] of Volos	jmg	[Frezis 2, 231]
Meshulam Pessah of Florina		[*lo nishkax* 18, 22]
Rabbi (Moissis) Mosheh Pessah	jmg	[Kabelli; Novitch, 143 Ben,
of Volos		Ch. 8; Frezis 2, 231]
'Petros' a Palestinian in charge		
of drop zone		[Kew, HS5//422]
Esdras Elia Philosof of Larisa		[E.M., *Larisa*]
Isaac Avraam (Yitzhak) P(h)ilosof		
of Larisa		[Ph. interview and book; AJM-C57]
Rafael Elia Philosof of Larisa		[E.M., *Larisa*]
Pinhas		[Ch. 2]
Morris Pinhas		[Ch. 2]
Haim Pinto		[AJM-C155]
Erikos Pipano of Salonika	jmg	[AJM-C157;Matsas, *Illusion*, 324]
Maurice Pipano		[AJM-C156]
Elias Politis of Volos		

[brother of M.P.]   **jmg**   [Frezis 2, 226]

Haim Politis of Volos   **jmg**   [AJM-ms; Novitch, 143; Ben, Ch. 8]

Moissis Politis of Volos   **jmg**   [Frezis 2, 226]

Albert Preznalis from Serres   **jmg**   [Ch. 1; Novitch, 143; Ben, Ch. 8; interview]

Yaakov Pulos   [AJM-ms]

Dora (Dorika) Raban   [03/9812]

Geoffrey Radcliff of G. B.   [Kabelli]

Y. Rapetis (?)   [Ben, Ch. 8]

David Raphael s. of Artaelo (?) of Ioannina   [AJM-C158]

Alhi Refael of Athens   [Ch. 6]

Leon Revi of Athens   [Besso's relative]

Avraam Romano of Salonika   [AJM-C159]

Ephraim Rosenberg of Salonika   [Kitsos]

David (Davico) Rousso of (Athens) Serres   **jmg**   [Ben, Ch. 8; ch. 4; AJM-C160 Matsas, *Illusion*, 273, 302;; 03/7254]

Isaac Rousso of Salonika [h. of Carmen Kakis]   [Kakis interview 7/26/03]

Jacob Rousso s. of Avraam   [AJM-C161]

Yitzhak Rousso of Serres   [*Routes of Hell*; ch. 2; interview; 03/7254]

Roza *andartissa* in Crete   [*Xronika*, vol. 27, #189 (Jan-Feb 2004), 17–19]

Simantov Rozen of Salonika   [Gila Hadar via Massua archive]

Dr. Sabetai   [AJM-ms]

Aaron Sabbetai of Volos [b of Raphael]   **jmg**   [Frezis 2, 226]

Minas Sabbetai (b)   **jmg**   [Frezis 1, 87]

Raphael Sabbetai of Volos   **jmg**   [Frezis 2, 226]

Israel Sadicario of Volos   **jmg**   [AJM-C162(!); Matsas, *Illusion*, 273]

Albert Safan   [d. Stella Safan]

Raul Saias		[Ch. 2; AJM-C166]
See Saki, Sakkis, Sciaki, Siaki		
Elli Sakki of Volos	jmg	[Frezis 2, 227]
Elias Sakkis of Volos	jmg	[Frezis 2, 226]
Eli Saki(a)s **Saki? Elias?**	jmg	[Novitch, 144; Ben, Ch. 8; Matsas, *Illusion*, 288]
Isaac Sakkis tou Aimilio of Volos		[Frezis 2, 231]
Joseph-Jacob Sakias of Volos	jmg	[Novitch, 143-4; Matsas,
and sister		*Illusion*, 287- **Salias**]
Leon Sakkis s. of Isaac	jmg	[br M.S.] [Ph. interview;
and Lea of Volos		Ch.1; Novitch, 144; Matsas, *Illusion*, 280; 03/8664]
Moissis Sakkis of Volos	jmg	[Ch. 1; Matsas, *Illusion*, 222;
'Prometheus'		Frezis, 226]
Pepos Sakkis of Volos and		
brother	jmg	[Frezis 2, 227]
Isaac Sakis of Larisa		[interview w/Shmuel Cohen]
Yitshak Saki [same as Isaac Sakis?]		[Kabelli]
Yosef Sakis and his brother [possibly		
same as Joseph-Jacob Sakias]		[Ben, Ch. 8]
Albertiko Sako of Kastoria		[Kastoria ,3]
Albert Salem of Salonika		[AJM-C168]
Mordecai Salem (b) of Salonika		[AJM-C167]
Saltiel		[Ch. 2]
Angel (Ansel)Saltiel		[AJM-C9]
Manolis Saltiel of Salonika		[AJM-C169]
Raoul Saltiel (service w/Force 133)		[Kew, HS5/398 #637]
Ioseph Samarias of Volos		[Frezis 2, 226]
Pepos Samarias of Volos	jmg	[Frezis 1, 87]
Menahem Sampatei (Sabetai)		[jewishpartisans.org]
David Samuel of Salonika		[AJM-ms; Matsas, *Illusion*, 272]
Albert Saoul		[AJM-C162]
Joe Saporata		ms of Yanni Megas (Captain Gregory) via Annette Fromm
Bouena Sarfatty of Salonika		*[Jewish Women, A Comprehensive Encyclopedia]*
Dr. Salvatot Sarfati (Crete)		[AJM-ms]
Sarika (see Sara Yehoshua)		[Ch. 3]

David Sasson	jmg	[Matsas, *Illusion*, 420]
Isaac Sasson		[AJM-C163]
Salomon Sasson	jmg	[Ch. 6; AJM-ms; Novitch, 144; Ben, ch. 8]
Iakov Savvas from Volos	jmg	[Ch. 1; R. Frezis, EMoyse, *Xronika*]
Itzhak Schiakim		[Novitch, 144]
Barukh Schibi of Salonika		[Kabelli, ch. 6; Novitch, 142; Ben, ch. 8; memoir]
Abraham Sciaki		[Ch. 5]
Salomon Sciaki	jmg	[AJM-ms; Novitch, 144; Ben, Ch. 8]
Yitshak Sciakis of Salonica		[Ben, Ch. 8]
Mosheh Segora ('Toto') of Salonika		[Ch. 1]
Serror [Cohen? female] of Salonika		[AJM-C164; Matsas, *Illusion*, 274, 324; *lo nishkax*, 16, 35]
Serror (JACK?)	jmg	[Matsas, *Illusion*,]
Shlomo Shenka		[Ch. 1]
Into Shimshi ('Makkabaios') of Salonika	jmg	[Ch. 4; memoir; AJM-C170]
Elias Siaki		[AJM-ms]
Isaac Siaki	jmg	[AJM-ms]
Jacob Siaki b. of Isaac of Volos		[AJM-ms]
Joseph Siakis s. of Jacob **See Sakias**		[AJM-ms]
Leon Siakis **See Leon Sakkis**		[AJM-ms]
Moissis Siakis		[AJM-C175]
Israel Sidarikis of Agrinion		[AJM-ms; Novitch, 143 – Saderakis; Ben, Ch. 8]
Sam Sidis of Athens	jmg	[Kabelli; Novitch, 144; Ben, Ch. 8]
David Soulam	jmg	[Novitch, 143; Ben, Ch. 8; brother of Leon? via Yomtov Mosheh]
Moris Stroumsa of Salonika in EPON		[Ch.1; Abatzopoulou, 1999, 118]
Abraam Svolis of Ioannina	jmg	[AJM-C171; Matsas, *Illusion*, 198, 311]

Emby Svolis of Ioannina		[Annette Fromm]
Ilias Svolis of Ioannia		[AJM-C172]
Michael Svolis of Ioannna		[Eliasif Matsas]
Yoseph Tabokh of Verroia		[03/5313]
Yoseph Nisim Taraboulous of Larisa	jmg	[Matsas, *Illusion*, p. 325; E.M., *Larisa*]
David Tiano of Salonika	jmg	[Novitch, 144; Ben, Ch. 8; AJM-C173; Matsas, *Illusion*, 272]
Zacharias Touron of Volos	jmg	[Frezis 1, 87]
David Tshuvah of Larisa		[Haifa conference]
Jacko Tshuvah of Larisa (son)		[Haifa conference]
Anjil Tsiako of Salonika		[AJM-C8]
Yoseph Tsis of Trikala		[EMoyse, *Xronika*]
Mihalis Valais of Ioannina		[Matsas, *Illusion*, 315]
Shimon Valestai of Athens		[Besso interview]
Avraam Varon of Kavala		[AJM-C14]
Max Varon of Kavalla		[Ben, Ch. 8]
Joseph Varouh (also see Auschwitz list)		[Ch. 7]
Saby (Sampetai) Varsano		[AJM-C15]
Eliyahu Veissi	jmg	[Kabelli; Novitch, 144; Ben, Ch. 8]
Alberto Vellelis of Patras		[Matsas, *Illusion*, 193]
Emmanuel Vellelis of Patras		[Matsas, *Illusion*, 193]
Zhak (Jacques) Ventura	jmg	[Kabelli ; Novitch, 144 ; Ben, Ch. 8]
Beraha Vital of Salonika [Peraha	jmg]	[AJM-ms]
Theophilos Vitalis of Volos	jmg	[Matsas, *Illusion*, 282; Frizis 2, 225]
Basilis Xazan of Salonika (dentist)		[Theo Pavidis]
Albert Yahbes of Kavalla	jmg	[03/2990; 03/2991]
Albertos Yahon of Salonika	jmg	[Matsas, *Illusion*, 325; 03/2990]
Stella Yahon of Salonika	jmg	[Matsas, *Illusion*, 325]
Yakoel of Kavalla		[03/8778]

Yomtov Yakoel of Trikala		[Kabelli, Ben, Ch. 8; EMoyse, *Xronika*]
Dr Yanni		[Afterword]
Sara Yehoshua ('Sarika') of Halkis	jmg	[Ch. 3; AJM-C165; Matsas, *Illusion*, 317; interview]
Aron Yerushalmi of Palestine		[Uris, *The Angry Hills*]
Albertos Yesoulas of Volos		[Frezis 1, 87]
Moissis Yesoulas s. of Elia of Volos	jmg	[AJM-C18; Matsas, *Illusion*, 324]
Iakob Yesouroum		[AJM-ms22]
Mois Yesouroum of Athens		[AJM-ms22]
Dr Moissis Yessurum of Ioannina	jmg	[Matsas, *Illusion*, photo; Ch. 4; Ben, Ch. 8]
[Mois Yessouroun		[AJM-C19; EMoyse, *Xronika*]
Pepo Yoseph		[*lo nishkax*, 16, 37]
Minas Zak of Volos		[Frezis 1, 87]
Ioseph Zakar of Volos		[Frizis 2, 225]
Avram Zhak of Kavalla		[Matkovski, 106]
Bezha Zion		[Matkovski, 106]

[total: 650]

Appendix II:
Auschwitz 2 (Birkenau) Sonderkommando Revolt, 7 October 1944

This list includes those known to have been in the Sonderkommando, who participated in the planning, who had a role assigned in the revolt, or who actually took part in the fighting. Estimates are that more than 300 Greek Jews in the Sonderkommando were among those preparing for the revolt. It is not known how many of the following were not in some way involved in the revolt, but it seems proper to err on the side of inclusiveness in recording any name that has survived that period. See Fromer, *Holocaust Odyssey*, 52, citing Martin Gilbert, *The Holocaust* (N.Y., 1985), 743, 889f for estimate.

Alex	(Webber, *Auschwitz: A History in Photographs* (Warsaw and Bloomington, IN, 1993, 42f, 172ff)
✡ Maurice Aron	(jmg; Matsas, *Illusion*, p. 246)
✡ Baruch Baruch	(b. Arta 1915)
✡ Isaac Barouch	(Novitch, p. 140; jmg)
✡ JosephBarouch	(Novitch, p. 140; jmg)
✡ Aaron Barzilai	(Fromer, *Holocaust Odyssey*, 77)
✡ Daniel Bennahmias	(Fromer, *Holocaust Odyssey*, 65)
✡ Matys Bitali	(b. Arta 1913)
✡ Jacob Broudo	(Matsas, *Illusion*, p. 249; Ben, p. 150)
✡ Henri Nehama Capon	(Steinberg, *The Jews against Hitler*, 307)
✡ Leon Cohen	(Fromer, *Holocaust Odyssey*, 60)
✡ Raoul Djahon	(b. Salonika 1919)
✡ Alberto Moissi Errera [Alekos Alexandrides]	(b. Larisa) (Fromer, *Holocaust Odyssey*, 52; Esdra Moyse, *Xronika-M-J*, 2000)
✡ Dario Gabai	(Fromer, *Holocaust Odyssey*, 65)

✡ Albert Gani — (b. Prevesa 1916; Matsas, *Illusion*, p. 246)
✡ Joseph Gani — (b. Preveza 1926)
✡ Moise Gani — (b. Preveza 1913; Matsas, *Illusion*, p. 246)
✡ Pepo Gani — (b. Preveza; Matsas, *Illusion*, p. 246)
✡ Albert Jachon — (Fromer, *Holocaust Odyssey*, 60)
✡ Joseph Levy — (Matsas, *Illusion*, p. 246)
✡ Samuel Levi — (b. Ioannina 1906)
✡ Sabetay Levis — (b. Istanbul 1910)
✡ Mois Levy — (b. Istanbul 1914)
✡ Michael Matsas — (b. Korfu 1909)
✡ Elia Mazza — (b. Ioannina 1902)
✡ Menasche — (Fromer, *Holocaust Odyssey*, 52n)
✡ Mechoulam, Eliezer — (b. Xanthi 1908)
✡ Abroum Meli — (b. Kavala 1902)
✡ Haim Misan — (b. Arta 1922)
✡ Moissis Misan — (b. Arta 1924)
✡ Albertos Misrachi — (b. Chios 1910)
✡ Mois Misrahis — (b. Chios 1911)
✡ Moissis Negrin — (b. Ioannina 1909)
✡ Dani Marc Nachmias — (Heinz Kounio)
✡ Yossif Namer — (b. Athens 1924)
✡ Marcel Nadjary — (b. Salonika 1917)
✡ Eugen Nakamoulis — (b. Istanbul 1904)
✡ Salomone Pinhas — (b. Salonika 1924)
✡ Isaac Samuel Rousso — (Matsas, *Illusion*, p.175)
✡ Selomo brothers — (Heinz Kounio)
✡ Moissis Serris — (b. Ioannina 1919)
✡ Samuel Sidis — (b. Trikala 1904)
✡ Isaac Soussis — (b. Arta 1902)
✡ Jacques Soussis — (b. Athens 1909)
✡ Moissis Sabbetai — (b. Arta 1909)
✡ Giosepos Sabas — (b. Arta 1912)
✡ Pesos Sabas — (b. Arta 1912)
✡ Savas Sabetai — (b. Trikala 1911)
✡ Albert Salvado — (Shmuel Raphael of Bar Ilan)
✡ Alberto Tzachon — (Heinz Kounio)
✡ Joseph Varouh — (b. Corfu 1910)
✡ Hugo Barouh Venezia — (Fromer, *Holocaust Odyssey*, 52, 59f)
✡ Isaak Venezia — (Matsas, *Illusion*, p. 249; Fromer, *Holocaust Odyssey*, 70; (Ben, pp. 150f)
✡ Mois Venezia — (b. Salonika 1921)

✡ Salomone (Shlomo)   (b. Salonika 1923; Fromer,
   Venezia   *Holocaust Odyssey*, 68)
✡ Menahem Zakar   (b. Patras 1918)
✡ Yosef Zakar   (b Arta 1924)

WARSAW REVOLT   AUGUST 1944

WYitshak (Iaasac) Arukh	[Ben, ch. 10; Matsas, *Illusion*, 262]
WMosheh Bensoure	[Ben, ch. 10; Matsas, *Illusion*, 261]
WAlberto	
WDavid Cohen	[Ch. 6]
WAlberto Giladi	
WLeon El Porto	
WAlberto Levi	[Ben, Ch. 10; Matsas; *Illusion*, 257]
WDario Levi	[Ben, Ch. 10; Matsas, *Illusion*, 261]
WMois	
WMois Meir	[Ben, Ch. 10]
WJesse Moissi	[Ch. 6]
WMoses (Morris) Negrin	[Matsas, *Illusion*, 261]
W	Saul Senior [1] [Matsas, *Illusion*, 259]
WHayyim Saltiel	[Ben, Ch. 10; Matsas, *Illusion*, 261]

NOTE

1. Saul Senior is recalled as a hero by a number of Greek slaves in Warsaw. The Germans hanged
   him for trying to escape some time before the revolt. Nevertheless, he deserves to be included in this list

Bibliography

This bibliography contains three sections: Jewish sources on the resistance in Greece; general studies on the Greek resistance; Greek assistance to Jews. The bibliography is for general reference and is not comprehensive of the works cited in the book.

JEWISH SOURCES ON THE RESISTANCE IN GREECE

It is a phenomenon worth mentioning that there is little reference to the Jews in the Greek resistance in Michael Molho and Joseph Nehama, *In Memoriam*, Salonika, 1948–1953 (reprinted 1975; expanded Hebrew version Jerusalem 1965; Greek version). It is also noteworthy that this volume, written in the immediate aftermath of the Holocaust, is still the basic reference text for scholars, despite the research published during the past half century. In addition to the lack of archival material in this important summary of the wartime experience, scholars have been generally loathe to address the rather strong opinions subsequently recanted by its authors. The *Bulletin of Judeo-Greek Studies* has been monitoring Greek Jewish bibliography for the past two decades.

Ben, Yoseph, *Yehudei Yavan ba'shoah vehitnagduth 1941–1944* [Greek Jews in the Holocaust and Resistance 1941–1944], Tel Aviv, 1985.
Bowman, Steven, 'Jews in Wartime Greece: A Select Annotated Bibliography,' in John O. Iatrides (ed.), *Greece in the 1940s. A Bibliographic Companion*, Hanover and London, 1981.
—— 'Evvia Portage: The Jews, ELAS and the Allies in Evvia, 1943–1944', *ΚΑΜΠΟΣ: Cambridge Papers in Modern Greek*, No. 11 (2003), pp. 1–24.
—— 'Granny, what did you do during the war?,' *Los Muestros*, no. 51 (June 2003), pp. 21–2.
—— 'Notes on the Jewish Military Reputation in Greece, 1914–1935,' *Newsletter of the Jewish Museum of Greece*, 31(1991), pp. 4–6.

—— 'Joseph Matsas and the Greek Resistance,' *Journal of the Hellenic Diaspora*,17 (1991), pp. 49–68.

Elmaleh, Avram, *Les Juifs de Salonique et la Résistance Hellénique*, Istanbul-Salonique, 1949.

Feldman, Y. (with S. Bowman), 'Love and war on Mount Olympus: Jewish Participation in the Greek Resistance', *Thetis*, 4 (1997), pp. 253–7.

Friedman, Philip, 'The Jews of Greece During the Second World War',*The Joshua Starr Memorial Volume*, New York, 1953, pp. 241–8. [Isaac Kabelli supplied him with Greek bibliography which I have not seen].

Kabeli, Isaac, 'The Resistance of the Greek Jews', *YIVO Annual of Jewish Social Science* VIII (1953), pp. 281–8 [use with caution].

Matsas, Joseph, 'The Participation of the Greek Jews in the National Resistance', *Journal of the Hellenic Diaspora*, 17 (1991), pp. 55–68.

Matsas, Michael, *The Illusion of Safety*, New York, 1997. Bibliographic essay by S. Bowman, pp. 421–8.

Moisses, Asher, 'Jews in the Army of Greece,' in J. Slotsky and M. Kaplan (eds)., *Jewish Soldiers in the Armies of Europe*, Tel Aviv, 1967, pp. 182–5; reprinted in *Zikharon Saloniki. Gedulatah vehorbanah shel yerushalayim debalkan* [Memorial for Thessaloniki. Grandeur and Destruction of the Jerusalem of the Balkans], ed. David Recanati, Vol. I, Tel Aviv, 1972 (in Hebrew). Vols I and II contain Jewish resistance memoirs.

Molho , Michael and Joseph Nehama, *Sho'ath Yehudei Yavan, 1941–1944* [The Holocaust of the Jews in Greece 1941–1944], Jerusalem, 1965, revised Hebrew version of *In Memoriam* (Salonika, 1948).

Novitch, Miriam, *Le passage des barbares. Contribution à l'Histoire de la Déportation et de la Résistance des Juifs grecs*, Paris, 1967; reprinted Ghetto Fighters House, 1982; *The Passage of Barbarians*, Hull, England, 1989.

Steinberg, Lucien, 'Greek Jews in the Battle against Nazism,' in M. Mushkat (ed.) *Jews in the Allied Forces in the Fight Against Nazism*, Merhaviah, 1971, pp. 327–31 (in Hebrew).

Yaacovi, Yohanan, 'The Road to Captivity: A Short History of the Palestinian Units which served in the campaigns of Greece and Crete in the Spring of 1941', MA thesis, University of Tel Aviv, 1976 (unpublished; text in Hebrew with English summary).

GENERAL STUDIES ON THE GREEK RESISTANCE

There are numerous memoirs in Greek conveniently listed with the political affiliations of the authors in Hagen Fleischer's useful bibliography 'Greece under the Axis Occupation' in John O. Iatrides (ed.), *Greece in the 1940s. A Bibliographic Companion*, Hanover and London, 1981.

Dorman, Menahem, *Milhemeth ha-ezrahim biyavan (Detsember 1944–Yanuar 1945)* [Civil War in Greece, December 1944–January 1945], Tel Aviv, 1945.

Eudes, Dominic, *Les Kapetanios. La guerre civil grecque de 1943 à 1949*, Paris, 1970; English edn London 1972; Greek edn Athens, 1975.

Fleischer, Hagen, *Stemma kai Svastika. E Ellada tes Katohis kai tes Anistasis* [Crown and Swastika, Greece of the Occupation and Resistance], Athens, 1995. The author has added a chapter on Jews to the Greek version of his political study of the wartime period.

Gerolymatos, André, *Guerrilla Warfare and Espionage in Greece 1940–1944*, New York, 1992.

Hondros, Louis, *Occupation and Resistance: The Greek Agony 1941–1944*, New York, 1983.

Iatrides, John O., *Greece in the 1940s: A Nation in Crisis*, London and Hanover, 1981.

Mazower, Mark, *Inside Hitler's Greece: The Experience of Occupation 1941–1944*, New Haven, CT, 1993.

Myers, E. C. W., *Greek Entanglement*, 2nd edn, Gloucester, 1985.

Seraphis, Stephanos, *Greek Resistance Army: The Story of ELAS*, London, 1978.

GREEK ASSISTANCE TO JEWS

Bowman, Steven, 'Could the Dodekanesi Jews have been Saved?,' *Newsletter of the Jewish Museum of Greece*, 26 (Winter 1989), pp. 1–2.

—— 'Greek Jews and Greek Christians During World War II', in *Remembering for the Future*, Conference Preprints, I, Oxford, 1988, pp. 215–21.

—— 'Jews in War-Time Greece', *Jewish Social Studies* (Winter 1986), pp. 46–62; reprinted in Robert Marrus (ed.), *The Nazi Holocaust*, Vol. IV, Westport, CT, 1990.

Constantinopoulou, Photini and Thanos Veremis (ed.), *Documents on* the History of the Greek Jews: Records from the Historical Archives of the Ministry of Foreign Affairs*, Athens, 1999.

Itzhaki, Solomon, 'Lights and Shadows in the Balkans', *Congress Weekly*, 12 January 1944, pp. 9–10.

Kitroeff, Alexander, 'Documents: The Jews in Greece, 1941–1944: Eyewitness Accounts,' *Journal of the Hellenic Diaspora* XII (1985), 5-32.

—— *War-Time Jews: The Case of Athens*, Athens, 1995.

Stavrianos, L. S., 'The Jews of Greece', *Journal of Central European Affairs*, 3 (1948), pp. 256–81.

The Jews and The Liberation Struggle, a report of the Central Committee of EAM on the Jews of Greece and the liberation struggle, unpublished, n.d. [1945?].

Synchrona Themata, no. 17 (1994), special issue dedicated to Greek Jews.

Index

Recently published by Vallentine Mitchell

From Thessaloniki to Auschwitz and Back: Memories of a Survivor from Thessaloniki
Erika Kounio Amariglio

Before the Second World War there was a thriving Jewish community for some 50,000 people in Thessaloniki, Greece. In 1943, under Nazi occupation, virtually the entire community was deported to Auschwitz extermination camp. That Erika Amariglio and several members of her family survived is due only to a series of coincidences, which started with the fact that they were on the first transport to Auschwitz, and of the 2,800 people on the train they were the only ones who spoke fluent German.

Erika Amariglio's story covers the period before the war in Thessaloniki, the German occupation and the gradual tightening of restrictions, the transportation, the two-and-a-half years that she and members of her family spent in Auschwitz, the long death march back to Germany, their escape to Yugoslavia, and the eventual reunion of the family in Greece. It concludes with the author's return to Auschwitz many years later as a delegate to an international conference on the Holocaust.

From Thessaloniki to Auschwitz and Back has previously been published in Greek (a third edition is currently in preparation), German, French and Serbia; a Hebrew edition is due to appear shortly.

Recently published by Vallentine Mitchell

An Anzac Zionist Hero:
The Life of Lt-Colonel Eliazar Margolin
Rodney Gouttman

Rodney Gouttman provides the reader with a groundbreaking biography of a quiet, engaging, and unassuming figure, a man of deeds rather than words. Eliazar Margolin participated in the primal foundation myths of two distinct nations, Australia and Israel. A pioneer farmer in Palestine whose exploits won the admiration of local Arabs, an original Anzac, a commander in the Jewish Legion before and after the Armistice of the First World War, he became, albeit briefly, the first Jewish military governor in the Holy Land for eighteen hundred years. An enduring feature of his personality was his concern and care for others, whether as a Zionist pioneer, with his Digger mates during the First World War, the Jewish Legion in the Holy Land, or as an active member of the RSL and Legacy in Perth. He was ever a soldier's soldier.

This narrative is thoroughly grounded in the national ands communal events of his day, including the Jewish Legion's great reward for the Anzacs, sharing a common hostility towards their British masters. 'Margy', as he was affectionately called, was buried twice, with full military honours, first in Australia and then in Israel. One enduring tragedy of his life was his exile from Palestine by the Mandate authority for his defence of Jewish immigrants during the Jaffa pogrom of 1921. Among those who crossed Elizar's path were Theodore Herzl, General Sir John Monash, Vladimir Jabotinsky, David Ben-Gurion, and Yitzhak Ben-Zvi. In Australia, his relationship was always tense and ambivalent, and on one occasion his character was falsely attacked by a misguided senator in the Australian Parliament.

Recently published by Vallentine Mitchell

Jews and Port Cities, 1590–1990:
Commerce, Community and Cosmopolitanism
David Cesarani and Gemma Romain (eds.)

With studies of Jewish communities in port cities ranging from sixteenth-century Livorno to modern Singapore, this book develops and extends the concept of the port Jew using a blend of conceptual innovation and original research. The first section explores the world of the Sephardi Jews, revealing patterns of mobility and networks that intertwined commerce, community and kinship. Individual case histories based on Livorno, Amsterdam, Curaçao, Charleston, Liverpool and Bristol examine how Jewish identity was formed in the unique milieu of the cosmopolitan maritime trading centre, how the commercial ethos of the bustling port promoted tolerance, and how the experience of civic inclusion was both a boon and a threat to Jewish life and culture. Innovative work on Hamburg, Corfu, Liverpool and Bristol also reveals that it was possible for intolerance to flourish in business circles and that competition could become a threat to ethnic diversity. Challenging research on Charleston and Liverpool shows how slavery cast a shadow over the Jewish population and created an environment of racialized identities in which Jews occupied an ambiguous and ambivalent position. The second section concentrates on the experience of Ashkenazi Jews in the modern era, when the port was less a commercial hub for exchange and more a location of production, transhipment and transmigration. Jews went from being primarily settlers and traders to becoming commodities in the business of mass migration. The studies of Libau, Cape Town, and Southampton show the importance of transmigration in the local and global economy and the limits of cosmopolitanism. A disturbing case study of Hamburg under the Nazis shows that a history of diversity was no guarantor of tolerance. Yet research on Glasgow, with its ethnic and religious fragmentation, shows how far Jews and non-Jews in port cities could get along functionally and amicably. All these contributions explore the concepts of diaspora and identity, probe the links between commerce and inter-communal relations, and map the subtle, shifting contours of language, culture and community in the unique mercantile environment in the world's greatest ports.